For Nupur and Arianne,
they love books,
and I love them.

Cover design, layout and interior illustrations and design by Alexandra Nereuta. http://cargocollective.com/alexnereuta

Additional graphic work by Nishant Sapra.

This edition July 2014, by OneWord Publishing LLC

For bulk orders, additional information, compliments and travel advice, visit www.gordoncasey.com or email Gordon.casey@frontshore.com

ISBN 978-0-9904364-0-9

the CAYMAN EDGE

HOW TO SET UP A CAYMAN FUND

GORDON CASEY

01

SETTING UP
A CAYMAN HEDGE FUND

02

KEY ISSUES
WORTH NOTING

03

APPENDICES:

INTRO DUC TION I

INTRODUCTION I
A Starting Point, and a brief FAQ

So, you want to set up a fund in the Cayman Islands? Here are the five steps: decide on a structure, incorporate the fund, prepare your documents, appoint your service providers, launch your fund.

Sounds simple right? Well, it is, actually, but the devil is in the details and with so much going on between so many people so far away, it's easy for a few things to go wrong and derail the entire project, or at least push your launch back by a few weeks or months, or go well over budget.

LET'S DIG INTO THE DETAILS...

Front Shore has set up over a dozen funds in the past couple of years. During that time, we have constantly refined the process and procedure. I'd hesitate to label our approach 'lean' management or 'kaizen' but we pay attention to those concepts and best practices and we're always tinkering and making incremental improvements to one or another aspect of the work that we do.

We primarily act as a project manager for fund setups;

establishing the offshore fund is a time-intensive process with a number of different tracks running simultaneously. We can take care of the structure while you focus on all of the other important aspects of actually launching the fund, like raising capital and putting everything into place to execute your strategy. We know the most likely places for delays to occur in the formation process and can help you establish aggressive, but realistic, timelines.

This book is intended as a guide to help anybody that is looking to set up a fund in the Cayman Islands, or is involved in the process in a tangential way and wants to get an idea of what is going on. We would love to be your actual guide, but in the absence of Front Shore directly, this book can be the next best thing.

The first half of the guide is written as a step-by-step document to be read sequentially. We start with the basics of the regulatory playing field in Cayman, then we move on to the players involved (the funds, the managers and the service providers); and then we look through the process (the documentation, the timelines and a detailed walk-through of a sample setup project).

We provide reasonable timelines for each activity as well as a summary Gantt chart of the entire process, including suggested responsible third parties for each activity. This is the same sort of tool that we use, but, obviously, is not tailored for your specific needs and counterparties.

In the second half of this guide, you'll find short chapters on various issues that have been,

are, or will soon be hot topics. Things like director's duties, FATCA and side letters (a perennial issue, it seems). Many of these topics are covered regularly in articles both online and offline, and these chapters should serve as a decent starting point for you to understand further developments and investigate any of these issues in more detail.

In addition to this guide, you can go to gordoncasey.com, the companion website where you can download some of the images and charts used in the book, some of the sample documentation we use for standard procedures such as appointing and removing directors, and active links to other online resources such as CIMA forms and so on (although we also provide links in the Resources Appendix).

We will also use this website to post updates in the event that any information changes after publication.

The appendices cover helpful information that you may want to access if you decide to go ahead with your fund: cost estimates and structures, online resources, service provider contact details, and so on.

A BRIEF NOTE ON STYLE:

this is not an academic treatise,

nor a legal paper or opinion

In fact, for the purposes of a disclaimer, you should treat this as if it's complete speculation! Naturally we've made our best efforts to ensure that this guide is accurate and up-to-date but our other primary goal was to write clearly, in plain English, and succinctly (you may no-tice that the chapters are short

— this is intentional. I have vigorously resisted efforts to expand the chapters merely to increase word count). You won't find sentences in here that say "The Mutual Funds Law (2012 Revision) of the Cayman Islands explicitly lays out the following criteria as applicable in the determination of whether the entity falls under the purview of the statute." But you will find stuff like "In Cayman, your fund will need to register with the Cayman Islands Monetary Authority if more than 15 people invest in the company."

A BRIEF NOTE ON TERMINOLOGY:

I primarily refer to companies, directors and shareholders in this Guide, and you may be more accustomed to think of funds as partnerships, or unit trusts.

I have chosen to refer to the company model because that is the most common form of fund in the Cayman Islands, but partnerships and unit trusts are used quite extensively there as well. I would therefore ask that when you read 'company,' you imagine that I am also referring to partnerships and unit trusts; when you read 'director,' you imagine I am also referring to the general partner and the trustee; and when you read 'shareholder,' you imagine that I am also referring to limited partners and unit-holders. It would just be too exhausting to read the convoluted sentences that would result if I had to insert all of the possibilities every single time I mention a structure or the investors and insert all the necessary "as the case may be"-type phrases. Of course, in instances where it is necessary or helpful to detail the differences that apply under different corporate regimes, I have done so.

LAST NOTE:

sometimes I capitalize the word Fund, Master, Feeder and so on, this is mostly a personal, whimsical thing, but it's also an indication that you can find a definition of that term in the glossary.

COMPANY
=
**PARTNERSHIPS &
UNIT TRUSTS**

DIRECTOR
=
**GENERAL PARTNER &
TRUSTEE**

SHAREHOLDER
=
**LIMITED PARTNERS &
UNIT-HOLDERS**

FAQ
SECTION

WHAT IS A FUND?

A group of investors get together, pool their money, and then invest it.

That's a fund. Sometimes referred to as a 'collective investment scheme,' a fund can take the form of a partnership, a company or an even more informal type of arrangement of some sort. The key element is the grouping of funds for a common investment purpose.

In the context of a hedge fund, the fund will be managed by someone other than the investors, so the investors provide the money and then a professional invests the capital on behalf of the fund (and, therefore, on behalf of those investors).

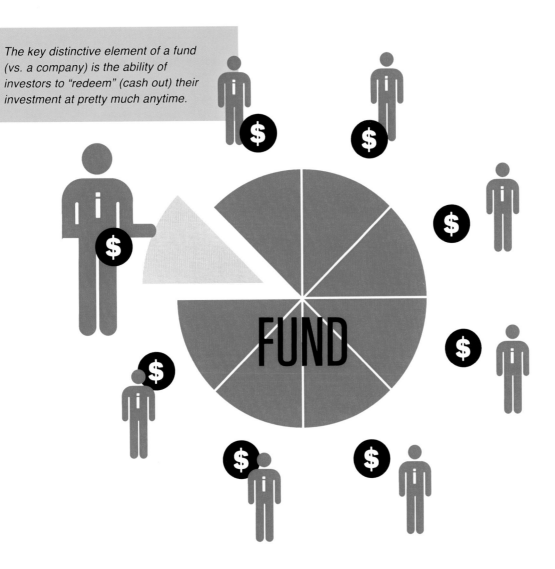

The key distinctive element of a fund (vs. a company) is the ability of investors to "redeem" (cash out) their investment at pretty much anytime.

HOW IS INVESTING IN A FUND DIFFERENT FROM INVESTING IN A REGULAR COMPANY?

One of the main differences between investing in a fund and investing in a company is that you cannot sell your shares in a fund to someone else.

Instead, if you wish to "sell" your shares, the fund promises to buy them back from you; this is what we mean when we say you "redeem" your shares — you just sell them back to the fund (see "What is a Redemption" below).

Note that this is similar, but different, to some of the common restrictions that apply when you invest in a private company — there is usually a shareholder agreement that will restrict your rights to sell your shares to third parties. Funds are different here, however, because most private companies do not promise to redeem your shares, or have an ongoing method to value your shares and the price at which they will be redeemed.

HOW DOES THE FUND DETERMINE WHAT IT WILL PAY ME FOR MY SHARES? WHAT IF I DON'T AGREE WITH THE PRICE THEY OFFER?

One of the other unique features of a fund is that the price of the shares is determined on an ongoing basis. When you invested in the fund, you promised that you agreed with the method that they were going to use to calculate the value of the fund. The way the value is calculated is via the net asset value, or NAV.

WHAT IS A NAV?

So, the fund's NAV is essentially the value of all of the fund's investments, less any expenses incurred or accrued, including the manager's fees. The NAV per share reflects how the NAV has changed from when you first invested — if you bought the shares at a NAV per share of $1,000, and now the NAV is $2,000, you know that the fund has increased in value by 100% since your initial investment.

ASSET

As the value of the underlying investments grows

initial value

growth in value

WHAT IS A
NAV?

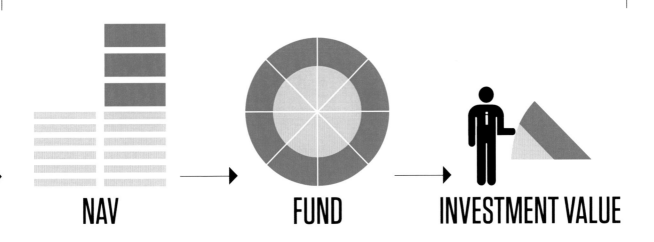

NAV

FUND

INVESTMENT VALUE

so does
the fund's NAV

and therefore
the size and value
of the fund

and the value of
each investor's
investment in the
fund

HOW OFTEN IS NAV CALCULATED?

The frequency of NAV calculation is generally also tied to when the fund will accept subscriptions and process redemptions. The most common period for NAV calculations is monthly, but quarterly, weekly and daily calculations are also common these days.

WHAT IS A SUBSCRIPTION?

A subscription is simply an investment into the fund. You 'subscribe' for shares rather than buy them because you submit an application for the purchase of the shares at a specific date in the future (the next NAV date, often referred to as a Dealing Day) — this is similar to the process used for public offerings and so the same terminology has been adopted.

WHAT IS A REDEMPTION?

In a normal company it is not common, and frequently not possible, for the shares in the fund to be re- purchased by the company. In a fund, this is exactly what happens, and this process is known as redemption.

The only way (pretty much) to 'sell' your shares is to sell them back to the fund via the redemption process. There tend to be some restrictions around redemptions relating to the notice period you must give, a minimum period of time for which you must hold the shares before you can redeem them (a 'gate' or 'lock-up') and the days on which shares may be redeemed (Dealing Days, or days on which the NAV is calculated — some funds only allow redemptions annually or quarterly, even though the NAV may be calculated more frequently.)

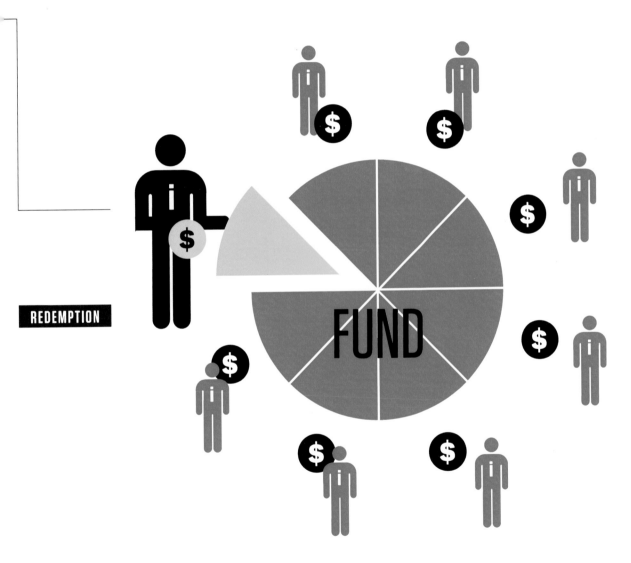

REDEMPTION

FUND

INTRO DUC TION II

INTRODUCTION II
Why Go Offshore?

Before you go any further, there's a cute little baby elephant in the room that we should address. Why you should setup your fund offshore in the first place. It has something to do with tax, you might be thinking, but you have no interest in avoiding legitimate taxation, so what's the story here? How come so many managers end up setting up an offshore fund in addition to, or sometimes instead of, an onshore fund?

One of the first things to realize is that your "onshore" is somebody else's "offshore." That's right! Wherever you live, that's an "offshore" jurisdiction to anybody who doesn't live in your country.

But you're not living in a tax haven, right? Well, probably not, given that the current

OECD (Organisation for Economic Co-operation and Development) definition of "tax haven" includes some fairly pejorative language. But the place where you live probably does have a lot of tax incentives designed to attract businesses, or investors, or specific industries such as film, mining, or eco-tourism.

Some of the biggest and most successful offshore (by which I mean: highly-tax-incentivized) locations are in regions that most people would call "onshore": London, the Netherlands, Canada, Delaware, Nevada, Ireland, etc.

Once you've wrapped your head around that, the next thing

you should consider is how you would feel if you decided that you, a tax-paying citizen of Taxland, wanted to invest in the fabulous fund that had been set up in Other tax land. But, lo and behold, when you go to fill out the subscription documents, you find that in order to invest, you're going to have to register as some sort of foreign excluded tax-payer in Othertaxland, too.

You may not have to pay any taxes, at least not right away, but you'll have to file reports every year that you hold the investment and for 5 years afterwards.

You'll also file reports here in Taxland, and if you ever redeem your investment, which, obviously, you want to do at some point, you're going to have a lot more forms to fill

out both here in Taxland and in Othertaxland. You start asking around for a lawyer who can give you some advice on this, and then it becomes clear that just making the investment and maintaining it is going to cost you a fair chunk of cash and the whole thing makes you feel a little queasy.

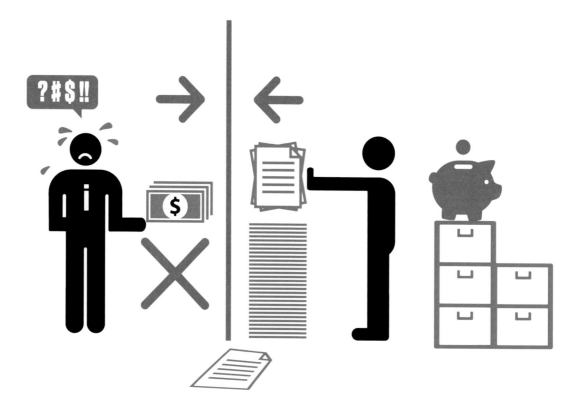

Ahh, how simple it would be if you could just invest your money in a fund that was set up in some utopian place where you wouldn't have to go through all of that hassle...

This is what we mean when we say that the Cayman Islands (and other offshore financial centers) are "tax neutral." The point is not to avoid tax, per se; it's to avoid foisting the tax regime of one or another specific jurisdiction onto investors and participants of another tax regime. I have, naturally, engaged in a bit of simplistic hyperbole here, but the point is valid and the regulatory burdens that would be applicable to certain investors are particularly egregious (but I don't want to pick on any specific tax authority here —
I think they're all equally guilty and hypocritical.)

The answer to the question "Why Go Offshore?" is: to facilitate investments from certain investors and reduce their individual regulatory burden. It is a simple matter of fact that, at this point in time, if you are trying to market your fund to certain specific investors with specific (and fully legitimate and legal) requirements, you will not stand a chance of raising any money unless and until you have a tax neutral fund in place through which they can invest.

CHAP
TER
ONE

CHAPTER 1

Cayman Funds 101

The Cayman funds regime envisages 6 different types of funds: exempted, registered, licensed, administered, public and, most recently, master. Each type of fund has different corporate and regulatory requirements associated with it (as well as certain requirements in common), and I want to outline both the definition of each type of fund and the requirements associated with each.

(Chapter Three contains a little flow chart to help you determine which regulatory regime, or regimes, is available for your situation and a summary of the obligations applicable to each is included at the end of this chapter.)

But before we go any further, we need to define the term Fund. The primary definition is familiar — a fund is any vehicle where investors pool money in order to make investments. I want to highlight one of the key exemptions from that definition: a fund is not a fund in the eyes of the Cayman Islands fund regulatory regime unless the shares in the fund are redeemable at the option of the investor. That means that a closed-ended fund is not, per se, a fund, and is not subject to the requirements laid out below. However, many closed-ended funds opt to register with CIMA (the Cayman Islands Monetary Authority, the main regulatory body in Cayman) primarily due to the benefits they obtain from being regulated by it.

CHECK OUT THE FAQ TO SEE WHAT IT MEAN FOR SHARES TO BE REDEEMABLE.

A closed-ended fund is a fund with shares that are not redeemable and will usually 'close' and return funds to the investors, together with the return on their investment, after an agreed period of time.

EXEMPTED FUND

An Exempted Fund has less than 15 investors and the majority of those investors can remove the directors of the Fund.

These funds are specifically exempted from the requirements of the governing legislation altogether (by Section 4(4) of the Mutual Funds Law, in case you want to look it up).

It is, for all intents and purposes, just like a company. It has to comply with the normal rules and regulations governing Cayman entities as a whole (such as the requirement to have a registered office and agent and to pay annual fees to the Companies Registrar), but none of the other requirements that we're about to look at will apply.

REGISTERED FUND

A registered fund, on the other hand, is a fund that is either listed on a recognized stock exchange or has a minimum investment amount of $100,000.

> *The minimum is actually 80,000 Caymanian dollars "or its equivalent in any other currency." The Caymanian dollar (KYD) trades at a fixed rate to the U.S.dollar 1.19, so the minimum is actually just over USD95,000.*

Registration with CIMA requires submitting some forms, your offering document, complying with the ongoing requirements laid out in the legislation (such as notifying CIMA of any material changes within 21 days), and paying the prescribed fee every year.

Registered Funds are required to be audited annually (see the sidebar on pages 26-27 on Cayman audits for more details).

While this does not constitute licensing in the way you might conceive of an SEC or FCA licensed body, the fund is still subject to the oversight of CIMA, which is the regulatory body in Cayman, and they can (and do) refuse or rescind a fund's ability to operate if they see fit.

LICENSED FUND

A Licensed Fund is a rather more complicated entity to establish, and probably more in line with what you would associate with the licensing regime found in the U.S. or the UK.

Under this regime, the fund is fully licensed by CIMA, subject to its approval of the documentation and the principal operators, administrators and promoters.

In practice, these funds tend to be offshore products by larger international operations, rather than the offshore sister fund of an onshore hedge fund manager.

In addition to the requirements of the funds legislation in Cayman, these funds may be subject to certain specific restrictions laid out within the license itself. It's worth noting that, unsurprisingly, licensed funds must also be audited by a Cayman Islands licensed auditor.

ADMINISTERED FUND

An Administered Fund uses a Cayman-licensed fund administrator as its registered office and notifies CIMA that it is operating as such (check out section 4(1)(b) in the Mutual Funds Law for the authority for this, and Form MF 2 on the CIMA website – details are in the Resources Appendix).

Once again, these funds must be audited and must notify CIMA of any changes to any of the information contained in the form that was submitted to it.

And the annual fees need to be paid, of course.

PUBLIC FUND

Like a lot of the other fund types that we've discussed here, (but this is a bit of legal nicety so I haven't really gone into it) the Public Fund, as a category, is more of an exception than a rule and, technically, it falls under the same definition as what we refer to as a Registered Fund.

The law says, simply, that a fund that is listed on a recognized stock exchange (there is a list of recognized stock exchanges available — check with your offshore lawyer if you want the latest) does not need to get a license.

But it does need to comply with all of the other requirements applicable to a Registered Fund: it needs to complete the forms, submit them together with the offering documents and payment to CIMA, and it needs to undergo an annual audit.

Perhaps most importantly, Registered Funds are required to be audited annually by a Cayman Islands based auditor, and filed within 180 days of year-end.

In practice, since this requirement was introduced, this often means that the audit is done onshore at the investment manager's office or the administrator's office, and the Cayman arm of the audit firm reviews the audit, signs off on it and submits it to CIMA.

In the past two years, however, Cayman audit firms have taken a more aggressive approach to their audits and a large part of the work involved in the actual audit is shifting to the Cayman auditor. Given that they ultimately shoulder the liability and responsibility, it is hard to find any fault in this.

The requirement to register Master Funds was introduced by CIMA in 2012 to cover those entities that act as the master fund in a master-feeder fund structure (see below). Essentially, if you have one or more investors that is a registered or licensed feeder fund (but, perhaps importantly, NOT an Exempted Fund), then you have a master fund.

"WAIT, WHAT IS A 'FEEDER FUND?'" YOU SAY.

Aha, well you might start to get a bit dizzy here, but a Feeder Fund is a fund that invests more than 51% of its assets into another fund. The illustration (right) might make it a bit clearer or not.

Unsurprisingly, master funds need to register (check out Form MF4), file all the required info, and pay the annual fees to CIMA in order to operate your master fund. And can you guess what else? Yup, that's right; you need to submit to an annual audit by a Cayman-based audit firm.

MASTER FUND

FEEDER FUND

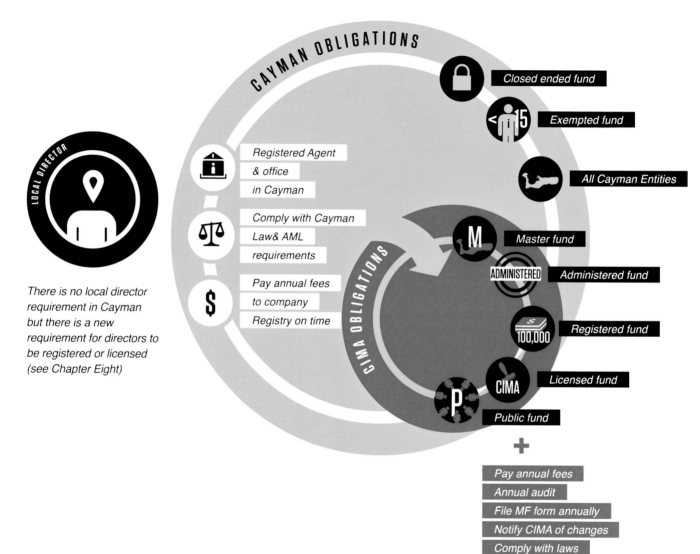

There is no local director requirement in Cayman but there is a new requirement for directors to be registered or licensed (see Chapter Eight)

CAYMAN OBLIGATIONS

CIMA OBLIGATIONS

Registered Agent & office in Cayman

Comply with Cayman Law& AML requirements

Pay annual fees to company Registry on time

Closed ended fund
Exempted fund
All Cayman Entities
Master fund
Administered fund
Registered fund
Licensed fund
Public fund

Pay annual fees
Annual audit
File MF form annually
Notify CIMA of changes
Comply with laws
Regulations & notes

ARE YOU A LEGISLATION JUNKY?

If you want to check out any of this in your own time, head on over to the CIMA website (see the Resources chapter) and look at the following sections in the Mutual Funds Law (you'll really impress your offshore-lawyer if you refer to the type of fund you want by section!)

s4(4)
Exempted Fund

s4(3)(a)(i)
Registered Fund

s4(1)(a)
Licensed Fund

s4(3)(a)(ii)
Public Fund

s4(1)(b)
Administered Fund

s4(3)(a)(iii)
Master Fund

CHAP
TER
TWO

CHAPTER 2
A Cayman Manager

Before we go any further, I would like to briefly describe the regulatory structure that governs the people or entities that act as the manager to the fund. This is the only chapter where I will touch on the details of this element of the structure. Forgive me for not going into the same level of detail as the rest of the book in terms of the entire setup process involved.

However, a lot of the timelines and processes applicable to setting up a fund are comparable to those that would apply to setting up an Investment Manager.

Although I will refer to the fund's manager as the investment manager, you may know him/her as the Investment Advisor or the General Partner (but do please note that the General Partner is not always the manager of the fund).

Under Cayman law, the definition of what exactly constitutes the activity of an Investment Manager such that you fall under their regulatory regime is long (5 pages of legislation). But we can generally say that if there is investment advice being provided, or will be provided, by an entity incorporated or registered in Cayman, then the activity will fall under Cayman regulation and we should consider what needs to be done in order to comply with the relevant requirements.

This will involve either a full licensing process or registration of an excluded manager.

LICENSED MANAGERS

In order to obtain a full license from CIMA, it will be necessary to file an application under the Securities Investment Business Law (SIBL) (the relevant form is Form SIBL).

The application has to demonstrate that the investment manager will comply with the legislation, will comply with all of the anti-money laundering ("AML") requirements applicable in the Cayman Islands, the management and shareholders are fit and proper persons, the staff are adequately trained, proper books and records will be kept, adequate insurance is in place, the company is financially sound, and there will be an annual audit performed. The license that is granted may be subject to certain conditions, such as the number of clients.

EXCLUDED MANAGERS

It is also possible to apply to CIMA using a different form (Form SIBL (AD)) to register as an Excluded Manager. In this instance, it will be possible to provide investment advice without undergoing a rigorous approval and licensing procedure — it is, in effect, the investment manager's version of the registered fund.

Here's how it works. You can apply to be registered as an Excluded Manager if, and only if, the investment manager is:

– Only providing advice to one or more companies within the same group of companies as itself; or

– Participating in a joint enterprise and the advice is only for the purposes of that joint enterprise; or

– Only providing advice to a Sophisticated Person, or people; or a High Net Worth Person, or people; or a company that is comprised of Sophisticated or High Net Worth Persons;

about Cayman Islands Dollars – so, KYD 80,000 or equivalent, which is roughly USD 100k).

We're going to get a little bit technical here but please bear with me. A Sophisticated Person is defined as (i) some-one regulated by CIMA or a recognized overseas regulatory authority; (ii) a company whose securities are listed on a recog-nized stock exchange; or (iii) someone who by reason of their "knowledge and experience in financial and business matters is reasonably to be regarded as capable of evaluating the merits of a proposed transaction" (see the definitions section of SIBL), and the transaction is worth at least USD 100,000 or its equiv-alent (once again, the statutory definitions here actually talk

A High Net Worth Person is someone whose net worth is at least USD 1,000,000 or who has total assets of at least USD 5,000,000 (technically, again, KYD 800,000 and KYD 4,000,000 respectively, but it's industry norm to convert that to USD and round up a little).

NEXT PAGE MORE DE-TAILS

SOPHISTICATED VS. HIGH NET WORTH PERSONS

Someone regulated by CIMA or a recognized overseas regulatory authority

Net worth is at least USD 1,000,000

A company whose securities are listed on a recognized stock exchange

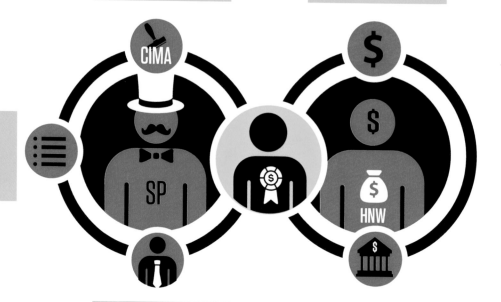

Someone who by reason of their "knowledge and experience in financial and business matters is reasonably to be regarded as capable of evaluating the merits of a proposed transaction"

Has total assets of at least USD 5,000,000

APPLICABILITY TO CAYMAN FUNDS

You may have noticed that the definition of a Sophisticated Person includes someone who is regulated by CIMA.

In case you're wondering whether or not that includes funds that are registered with CIMA but not licensed by them, the answer is yes — all categories of fund qualify as a Sophisticated Person for the purposes of SIBL, and so any investment manager to any of those funds may apply to be an Excluded Manager.

REGISTRATION PROCESS

If you're going to go ahead and register as an Excluded Person under SIBL, you will need to complete the form (SIBL(AD)) supply all of the requisite documentation, pay the registration fee, file an annual declaration that the details are still the same, and pay the annual fee (as of 2014, that's USD 6,098, on registration, and the same every year thereafter), and you would also need to appoint a Money Laundering Reporting Officer (MLRO).

CIMA may also require the Excluded Manager to undergo an audit.

If you are familiar with the US legislation and definitions, you may be experiencing a bit of déjà vu. In case you have noticed, yes, the Sophisticated Person and High Net Worth Person defi-nition under Cayman law are similar to the definition of Qualified Purchaser under s3(c)(7) of the Investment Company Act of 1940 and the definition of Accredited Investor under the Securities Act of 1933

I can assure you that it is completely intentional. While it's not a complete match, offshore fund regimes are always paying close attention to their onshore counterparts and the regulatory and legislative developments taking place there. This is both to stay on top of best practices and to ensure that they don't impose burdens any greater than those that are imposed "at home."

CHAP TER THREE

CHAPTER 3
Decisions, Decisions

Decisions, Decisions – Let's go through the CIMA Fund Regulation flow chart! There are a couple of key questions you can answer to determine which regulatory structure is available as an option for your fund. You may choose to launch a registered fund even if your fund meets the criteria to be exempt from registration, of course, but this little flow chart will help you determine which options are available to you.

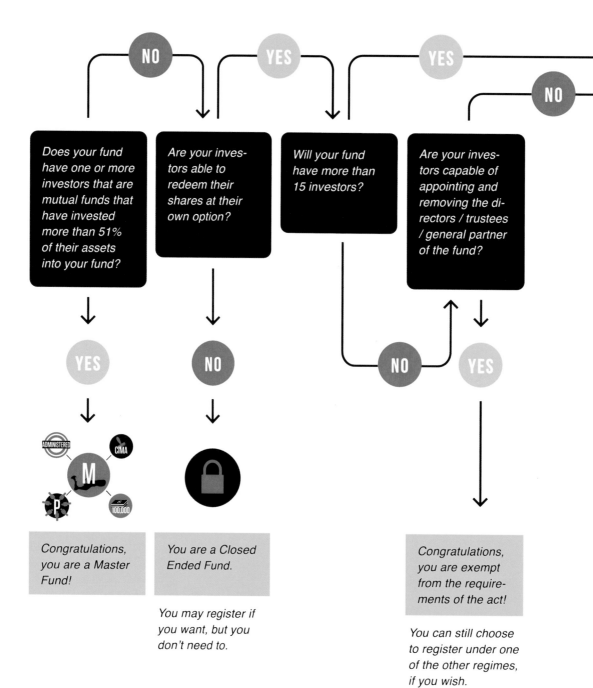

NO

YES

YES

NO

Does your fund have one or more investors that are mutual funds that have invested more than 51% of their assets into your fund?

Are your investors able to redeem their shares at their own option?

Will your fund have more than 15 investors?

Are your investors capable of appointing and removing the directors / trustees / general partner of the fund?

YES

NO

NO

YES

Congratulations, you are a Master Fund!

You are a Closed Ended Fund.

You may register if you want, but you don't need to.

Congratulations, you are exempt from the requirements of the act!

You can still choose to register under one of the other regimes, if you wish.

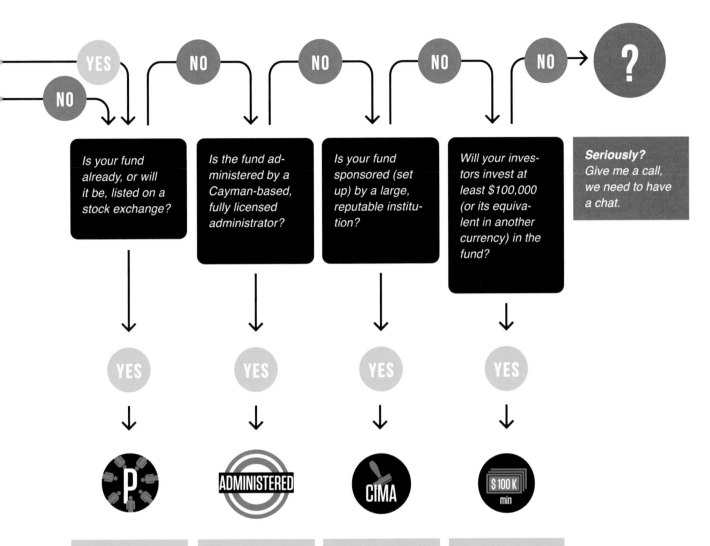

YES

NO

NO

NO

NO

NO

?

Is your fund already, or will it be, listed on a stock exchange?

Is the fund administered by a Cayman-based, fully licensed administrator?

Is your fund sponsored (set up) by a large, reputable institution?

Will your investors invest at least $100,000 (or its equivalent in another currency) in the fund?

Seriously?
Give me a call, we need to have a chat.

YES

YES

YES

YES

Congratulations, you are a Public Fund!

Congratulations, in cooperation with your Administrator, you may register as an Administered Fund!

Fantastic, you may be eligible to receive a full license from CIMA, if you qualify. At their discretion, you will be a Licensed Fund!

Fantastic! You've made it; you're a Registered Fund!

CHAP TER FOUR

CHAPTER 4
Service Providers 101

If you've been hunched over a Bloomberg terminal for most of your working life, you might not be familiar with the many (many) parties that are involved in keeping a fund ticking over on a daily basis.

Although technology has evolved substantially in the past decade to take care of a lot of the functionality provided by these service providers, they still provide true value to any fund (and its investors) and great care should be taken in choosing the right partner for the particular needs of your fund.

This chapter is intended to give you a brief introduction to seven of the key players involved in the set up and continuing operation of the fund. Where possible, I've tried to give some indication of the characteristics you should pay attention to when choosing whom to partner with, as well as how the contractual and pricing structure usually works for a given service provider.

We highly recommend that you use a lawyer to review all contracts the fund enters into with each service provider.

In certain cases, a number of these functions might be provided by a single group (although likely by different corporate entities within that group). But for the sake of clarity on the distinct functions being provided, I've written this as if it is handled by different people in each instance. There's an appendix at the back with a list of firms for each these headings.

FUND ADMINISTRATORS

This team will provide the backbone of the back office of the fund. In all likelihood, they will be responsible for calculating and distributing the Net Asset Value (NAV) on a regular basis. (Daily, weekly, monthly and quarterly NAV's are all common and depend entirely on the needs of the investment manager and the investor base).

A third-party independent fund administrator is critical to providing assurance to investors that the investment manager isn't just making up the performance figures as he goes (which, let's face it, has happened in the past — see appendix VII for more on knowing your hedge fund scandals).

Administrators typically also deal with shareholder relations (sending out offering documents, receiving subscription forms, keeping all of the due diligence information, processing redemptions) and, in the specific instance of the Administered Fund in Cayman, the Administrator will act as the registered office and agent of the fund.

The agreement with the administrator will specify the terms of their engagement, exclusions from liability, the list of services they will provide and the cost to do so, usually calculated (and payable) monthly on a minimum basis and then as a number of basis points of the total NAV of the fund, ranging from 4 to 16, depending on the complexity of the fund, the frequency of the NAV reports, the number of investors and the assets under administration.

PRIME BROKERS AND CUSTODIANS

It's kind of hard to overemphasize the importance of the Prime Broker's relationship with the fund and the investment manager. They can do the trades, provide leverage, act as the custodian of the fund's investment and even provide capital introduction services.

All said, this is a key, and ongoing, relationship, and it's imperative that you find the right partner from the outset — a prime broker who fully understands your strategy, your plans and your needs, both now and as the fund grows and succeeds.

Your contract with your Prime Broker actually could be a multitude of contracts, each one covering the different services that you require, or a contract bundle of sorts. While you may not, for example, need leverage on day one, if you expect that you will in the future, you should be talking about it now, discussing the terms, and starting to review documentation and contracts.

OFFSHORE LEGAL ADVISORS

No matter what sort of fund structure you end up utilizing for your Cayman fund, it's always wise to get reliable local legal advice. Hopefully this guide has helped you to identify the most likely path you will take and has put you in a position to move forward efficiently with a relationship with a law firm, but it is not, and does not pretend to be, a replacement for a good lawyer.

The Cayman Islands arguably have the best fund lawyers in the world. The majority of partners at the law firms there have practiced in more than one other jurisdiction and are, accordingly, extremely well placed not just to advise you on Cayman law, but also to offer a wide view of best practices globally, as well as more information on comparative fund regimes. They are also quite likely to understand the onshore regulatory regime in which you are based.

It is worth noting that the lawyers will act for the fund but that they do so on the instruction of the investment manager, (frequently referred to as the Sponsor, in this context), to begin with. They do not act for investors, and the fund documentation will usually include a disclaimer to that effect. This is a perennial issue of contention, due to the potential for a conflict of interest, and it's possible that we may soon see funds being set up with one set of lawyers to represent the fund and another set of lawyers to represent future investors (to a certain extent, this already happens where there is a major seed investor involved in the setup of the fund).

At the very least, however, there is now a sufficiently wide range of legal talent across the firms on the island that funds, investment managers and investors should all be able to appoint extremely qualified lawyers without running into any further conflicts.

REGISTERED OFFICE AND AGENT

Cayman, similar to most jurisdictions, requires that all companies incorporated there or operating there appoint a local party to represent the vehicle and be accountable to the Caymanian authorities. This service is provided by management companies, often run as sister companies of law firms or administrators.

The Registered Office will represent the fund both for its annual company filings with the Company Registrar and for any filings and correspondence with CIMA.

The agreement with the Registered Office will specify the nature of their service and the price; it will usually also mention the annual fees due to the Companies Registrar to maintain the company in good standing, as well as the cost to produce various documents that will be required throughout the life of the fund (copies of the Certificate of Incorporation, Certificate of Good Standing, etc).

The total cost per year is hard to estimate, as there are usually hourly costs charged as well, but it will be in the region of USD 1,500 as a minimum and can go as high as USD 5,000 or USD 40,000 if the Registered Office is required to do a lot of work on behalf of the fund in a given year. Some management companies will agree on an all-inclusive fee without additional hourly rates, but with disbursements (to the Company Registrar, courier costs, notarial fees) excluded.

AUDITOR

The auditor of the fund will be responsible for producing a timely audit report, which will need to be filed in Cayman for most funds (the exceptions, as discussed previously, are funds that aren't registered with, or licensed by, CIMA). Unsurprisingly, the more complicated the fund's strategy, the more expensive and lengthy the audit process.

It is quite standard these days for the fund to be required by the audit firm to sign an extensive representation letter confirming that all relevant information has been provided to the auditor. It is a good idea to agree a standard form of this letter upon appointment of the auditor rather than negotiate changes to the standard letter on a case-by-case basis over the years.

Audit fees for a Cayman fund cover the whole gambit and are a reflection of both the auditor chosen and the complexity of the work involved in the audit.

Historically there were only a few firms that had the requisite expertise in-house to perform an audit, but that is no longer the case, and most international audit firms are sufficiently familiar with the various fund structures and strategies to be readily capable of handling the vast majority of funds. That said, there are one or two firms with a broader depth of experience and they, generally speaking, charge a premium.

Fund audits can be as expensive as USD 100,000 for a stand-alone fund, but you should generally expect to pay between USD 15,000 and USD 40,000 in year one. While it may be tempting, particularly in the first year when revenue is

low, to go with the cheapest quote you get, bear in mind that this is a relationship that will, ideally, persist throughout the lifecycle of the fund. It is a worth a premium to find an auditor that understands not just your strategy, but also your way of thinking and working.

INDEPENDENT DIRECTORS

Historically speaking, offshore directors were appointed primarily to ensure that the fund was not deemed to be an onshore vehicle by the onshore tax authorities (mind and management were, therefore, kept offshore to the greatest extent possible). As litigation and losses started to hit some funds,

however, the expertise and fees of those directors increased, and their role is changing.

There are two common models of Independent Director available for Cayman funds. One is the fully independent, non-executive position, usually provided by an individual in a similar style of service as you might expect from a non-executive director at any listed company or perhaps a mutual fund. These directors either act completely alone or within a collection of similar individuals operating as a group in much the same way as a traditional legal partnership would.

The second model is the full service, independent-directors-as-a-business model. In this instance, you have a number of individuals that act as the actual directors but the primary value is driven by the large infrastructure backing them up, ensuring that documentation is kept in order, meetings are held on time and the fund is proactive in staying on top of regulatory developments within the industry.

Unsurprisingly, there is a third model that can fall anywhere in the range between the first and second models, and a number of funds will appoint one independent director from each model, effectively getting the best of both worlds.

The median fee payable to Independent Directors these days is somewhere around USD 15,000 and is steadily increasing. There is, however, a wide range of options, starting at around USD 7,500 for a highly cost-effective director but curving sharply upward thereafter, with a long tail up to fees as high as USD 80,000.

The director is appointed via agreement or letter and should specify the expectations of the directors, the length of their appointment, and the annual fee to be paid in return. Note that in order for the fund to take advantage of the exempted fund option, a majority of the investors must be able to appoint or remove the directors of the fund.

Please see chapter 8 for a discussion on the recently introduced legislation governing director services in Cayman.

INVESTMENT MANAGER

In the majority of Cayman funds, all the investment decisions have usually been delegated to the Investment Manager, who is frequently also the sponsor of the fund. While absolute responsibility for those decisions rests with the fund itself (and its board of directors), the fund's performance depends almost completely on the Investment Manager's ability to deliver on the strategy detailed in the

fund's offering documents.

The Investment Management agreement will specify the role of the Investment Manager, the terms under which the contract can be terminated (usually quite difficult), the fee to be paid, and how and when it is calculated — usually a 1-2% management fee, calculated and paid based on the total assets under management, and a 10-20% incentive fee, calculated and accrued monthly based on performance of the fund from previous high-water marks.

There are, however, many other methods for calculating the fees payable to the Investment Manager and, in addition to those laid out in the agreement, they should be laid out in explicit detail in the Private Placement Memorandum (or "PPM") so that all investors understand how the Investment Manager is compensated and incentivized.

It's worth noting that the Investment Manager may also sub-contract some or all of the investment decisions to an external advisor.

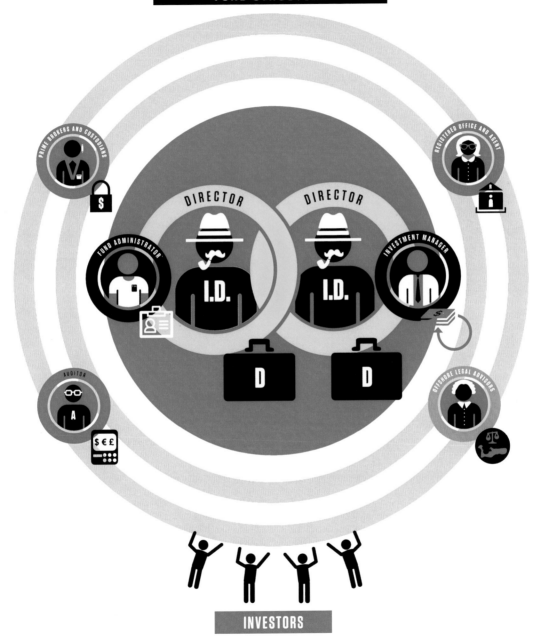

FUND STRUCTURE

PRIME BROKERS AND CUSTODIANS

REGISTERED OFFICE AND AGENT

FUND ADMINISTRATOR

DIRECTOR

DIRECTOR

INVESTMENT MANAGER

I.D.

I.D.

D

D

AUDITOR

A

OFFSHORE LEGAL ADVISORS

INVESTORS

CHAP TER FIVE

CHAPTER 5
Documentation 101

There is a wealth of paperwork involved in getting your fund up and running, and a wealth of terminology surrounding that paperwork as well. This chapter gives you a quick breakdown of the terminology, and the essential function and form of the documents. As mentioned in the introduction, our companion website (www.gordoncasey.com) contains samples of some of the documentation for you to use.

Naturally, the agreements with the service providers are a crucial part of the fund's operations as well, so consult Chapter Four if you need more information on those.

THE PRIVATE PLACEMENT MEMORANDUM

This document goes by many names, and each industry or jurisdiction usually has one phrase that constitutes the norm. It can be the Private Placement Memorandum, PPM (which is what I'm going to call it from now on), Offering Memorandum, Offering Memo, OM, Offering Document, Off Doc Prospectus... you get the picture.

This document is the fund's key document from a legal and regulatory point of view. It will identify the investment strategy, the structure being used, the various parties involved in the fund and the price and terms of their appointment, the risks inherent in the investment strategy, disclaimers against losses, and the terms and conditions of subscriptions and redemptions for all investors (and the terms of different offerings in the event of separate share classes).

Unlike the presentations that you will use on the road show, this tends to be a very long and dry document and should be meticulously scrubbed by your Cayman law firm.

Here is a list of questions that will need to be addressed during the process of drafting the PPM. Some will be quick decisions and some will raise more questions.

▼

A lot of these are discussed elsewhere in this guide, but this is a good starting point (there are other, obvious, questions that need to be answered, such as 'Who will be the fund's service providers?'):

1. WHAT TYPE OF CORPORATE STRUCTURE WILL THE FUND USE?

2. WILL THERE BE NON-PARTICIPATING VOTING SHARES?

3. WILL THERE BE DIFFERENT CLASSES OF PARTICIPATING SHARES?

4. WHAT WILL CONSTITUTE A QUORUM FOR SHAREHOLDER MEETINGS?

5. HOW FREQUENTLY WILL INVESTORS BE ABLE TO SUBSCRIBE AND REDEEM?

6. WILL THERE BE A LOCK-UP PERIOD FOLLOWING SUBSCRIPTION?

7. CAN THE FUND IMPOSE REDEMPTION GATES? UNDER WHAT CIRCUMSTANCES?

8. UNDER WHAT CIRCUMSTANCES CAN THE FUND SUSPEND SUBSCRIPTIONS AND/OR REDEMPTIONS?

9. UNDER WHAT CIRCUMSTANCES CAN THE FUND FORCIBLY REDEEM INVESTORS?

10. CAN THE FUND PAY OUT REDEMPTION PROCEEDS IN KIND?

11. HOW, AND HOW FREQUENTLY, WILL MANAGEMENT AND PERFORMANCE FEES BE CALCULATED AND PAID OUT?

12. HOW WILL THE HIGH WATER MARK OPERATE?

13. **WILL THERE BE ANY HURDLE RATE OR BENCHMARKING APPLIED TO THE FUND?**

14. **ARE THERE ANY SUBSCRIPTION FEES?**

15. **ARE THERE ANY REDEMPTION FEES?**

16. **WILL THE FUND HAVE A SIDE POCKET STRUCTURE AVAILABLE FROM INCEPTION?**

17. **WILL THE FUND PARTICIPATE IN NEW ISSUES?**

18. **WILL THE FUND ACCEPT ERISA INVESTORS?**

19. **WILL THE FUND USE DIFFERENT SERIES OR TRADITIONAL EQUALIZATION ACCOUNTING?**

20. **HOW WILL ASSETS BE VALUED?**

21. **WHAT ACCOUNTING SYSTEM WILL BE USED?**

DOWNLOAD A COMPLETE CHECKLIST FROM THE RESOURCES SECTION ON THE WEBSITE

(WWW. GORDONCASEY.COM)

SUBSCRIPTION DOCUMENT

Another very dry document, this is the form that must be completed and submitted by all investors. Technically speaking, it's the contract that binds the investor to the terms outlined in the PPM.

It will specify a few additional details of the offering, state that the investor has read and understood the PPM, and will also ask various questions to ensure that the investor is qualified to invest in the fund, as well as request various pieces of documentation to fulfill the anti-money laundering (AML) and know-your-customer (KYC) requirements that must be completed in order to satisfy the anti-money laundering obligations of all of the parties involved.

Different types of investors will usually complete different Subscription Documents based primarily on where they are investing from — the primary distinction in Cayman funds usually comes down to whether you are a non-U.S. investor, an exempt U.S. investor, or a U.S. investor. In light of recent changes in European regulatory governance, it is likely that we will see an increase in Subscription Documents drafted specifically for European investors (see Chapter 16 on AIFMD).

MEMORANDUM AND ARTICLES OF ASSOCIATION

We're developing a trend here: these are also pretty dry. However, these are the sine qua non of a corporate entity, the constitutional documents that create the fund itself (assuming you are using a limited liability company).

The Memorandum of Association can be thought of as an externally looking document (describing to outsiders what it is that the company is and does), whereas the Articles of Association can be considered internally focused (describing to the people operating the company how things are supposed to be done). The Mems and Arts (see what I did there?) of the fund are the starting point for any of the terms of the offering and the powers of the board and rights of shareholders of the fund.

It is crucial that the terms, as outlined in the PPM, and the conditions of the investment, as specified in the subscription documents, match what is contained in the M&A's (I'm doing it again, see – people are going to use all sorts of abbreviations for these documents, interchangeably and inconsistently, be warned!); they don't need to repeat everything, but they shouldn't contradict one another.

Another great reason to get a Cayman lawyer on board as soon as possible is to ensure that your documents cross-reference each other accurately.

PARTNERSHIP AGREEMENT

So, if you have established your fund as a Trust instead of a limited liability company, a lot of the terms that would be contained within the Memorandum and Articles of Association will instead be contained with the Partnership Agreement (also known as the Limited Partnership Agreement). The main party to the agreement will be the General Partner who is sometimes, but not always, also the investment manager to the Fund.

The General Partner is almost always the substance behind the partnership in the sense that they will provide the executive function and perform the work that must be done in order for the partnership to operate at all. In that sense they are analogous to the board of directors. Increasingly of late, due to the lack of formal governance structures inherently in place in a partnership structure, boards of advisors are being appointed to partnerships to provide the independent oversight that a board of directors would provide to a company.

LAUNCH RESOLUTION

A fairly brief and simple document, the launch resolution will proudly state the company's intention to register, or not, with CIMA, to become a fund in general, to appoint auditors, open bank accounts, issue shares and generally get on with it. It grants the directors (and usually any one of them) the authority to complete all the forms and do all the things that need to be done to get the show on the road. We've included an example for download on www.gordoncasey.com on the Resources page.

MF1, MF2, MF4

The MF series of forms are the forms that CIMA requires you complete in order to register your fund. The appropriate form must be completed depending on what sort of fund you are registering, and it includes the basic information regarding the offering being made as well as the parties involved with the fund. An authorized representative of the fund must sign the form.

The form will also need to be submitted with various pieces of supporting documentation, such as the PPM, the subscription documents and the consent letters (see below). Links to the forms are provided on the website and sample completed forms are available in the Template Documents appendix and on the website.

AUDITOR AND ADMINISTRATOR CONSENT LETTER

Prior to registering the fund with CIMA and filing the relevant MF form, you will need to obtain a letter of consent from both the proposed auditor and administrator of the fund. Sample letters are attached in the appendix for information purposes but, naturally, your administrator and auditor will have templates on file themselves.

FORM SIBL AND FORM SIBL(AD)

As mentioned in Chapter Two, if you are going to register an investment manager for a license, or for exclusion, you will need to complete the relevant form, prepare the supporting documentation, and submit it all to CIMA for approval.

We haven't covered investment managers in extensive detail in this guide, but we have included links to the original forms on the companion website, together with sample completed forms for you to use.

OTHER KEY RESOLUTIONS

Depending on the nature of your fund structure, it may be necessary to have other resolutions in place prior to the launch of the fund as well. Examples include the transfer of the first share from the incorporator to the first shareholder (frequently voting, non-participating "management shares" issued to the investment manager); the appointment of the first directors might also be contained in a separate resolution; and, in the case of Segregated Portfolio Companies, the creation of the portfolios might be contained in separate resolution, too.

We haven't included any of these in our appendix, but the website has quite a few templates that you can use prior to launch or during the life of the fund, including the resolutions mentioned above and documentation relating to resignation of board members, opening of bank accounts, waiver of redemption and subscription notice periods.

KEY SERVICE PROVIDER AGREEMENTS

These were discussed in more detail in Chapter 4, but for the sake of completion I'm including them here as well. These documents include the Administration Agreement; the Investment Management Agreement and possibly an Investment Advisory Agreement; the terms of appointment of the directors; the terms of appointment of the auditors; the Registered Office Agreement; and the Custody Agreement.

WHAT ABOUT ALL THAT KYC?

This is addressed more extensively in Appendix V – AML and KYC (which you should definitely have a look at), but we should talk about the documents that clients need to provide in order to comply with the know-your-customer (KYC) rules that form part of the anti-money laundering (AML) obligations under both Cayman law and internal policies for most service providers.

The primary obligation here is to establish the identity of the investors and to satisfy lawmakers that the funds are not tainted by any illegal activity. There are standard procedures involved in going through that process, which most service providers will insist on complying with: any copies of documents must be certified or notarized; some form of proof of address must be provided, along with proof of identity; somebody must provide a reference letter for you, and that person must somehow be independently accountable in a way that providing a false reference would have negative consequences for that person (so, a lawyer, judge, police officer, bank officer, accountant, etc.).

Note that there are extra obligations that will come into play if the investor is a Politically Exposed Person (PEP).

These generally just mean more extensive checks on the source of income and so on, but some funds will not accept these investors.

And lastly the goal of compliance officers all over the world is to get an individual's name associated with an account. So while the investment might be in the name of a company or another entity, which may be owned by a trust, which is part of another estate planning mechanism... ultimately, they want to trace the funds back to a person.

CHAP TER SIX

CHAPTER 6
Timelines and Expectations

We once set a fund up in a month. Well, most of it — by the end of the month, everything was done, except the broker account was delayed due to KYC issues. For reasons unknown, this led the client to delay the fund launch for over two years and eventually wind up the entire structure.

The problem is not that a fund is an especially complicated structure to set up (nor is it a piece of cake) but, in the majority of cases, most sponsors or managers have not established a foreign corporation before, nor have they been obliged to define and formalize all of the essential relationships of a business from day one.

But do not be fooled by service providers that tell you it is easy, or that it will only take a couple of weeks and not much of your time. Unless you have resources in-house that can dedicate themselves to the task, it may well prove frustrating, swallowing up time you would rather spend focused on your onshore fund, capital-raising or any of a myriad of activities required to execute your strategy properly from day one.

The truth is that establishing a Cayman fund is a time-intensive process involving multiple parties with a variety of deliverables and milestones. If you haven't done it before, it's hard to know what constitutes a reasonable expectation in terms of turn-around times, and it's impossible to know where to expect bottlenecks or which activities pose the greatest risk in terms of derailing the project, the budget or the timelines.

Our business at Front Shore is actually built around solving these problems. Front Shore acts as a project manager for fund setups; we start by establishing a realistic and acceptable timeline with all parties, clearly demarking responsibilities from day one, through each step until launch, helping the fund hit the ground running.

milestones, and the 3 greatest risks — all set out together with slightly generous timelines (it can certainly be done faster than this, but it shouldn't take much longer than this unless something goes wrong).

We know where the bottlenecks tend to occur, we know where the greatest risks are, and we can help take steps to avoid or mitigate them before they threaten the viability of the process as a whole.

We stay fully involved in the granular details of the project, scrutinizing each interaction to ensure that we're on track and no one misses a beat.

In the next chapter we'll walk you through a standard fund setup so you'll get to see the 6 basic tracks involved in a standard fund setup, the 5 key

CHAP TER SEVEN

CHAPTER 7

What to Expect When You're Expecting a Cayman Fund

I'd like to walk us through the entire setup process of a Cayman fund. We'll be making a few assumptions and decisions here about the structure, minimum investments, the strategy, and so on.

We're also going to assume that nothing really goes wrong. This is, of course, a far cry from reality and the real challenge in the process is spotting potential problems on the horizon and preempting them. Key areas of risk are identified throughout this chapter.

TRACKS

We work on the basis that there are six key tracks to the fund setup, plus a closing track for the Project Manager. In this chapter our text precedes a Gantt chart for the whole project. The Gantt chart is included on the website in a version that you can download and play around with. When you see the whole chart, the dependencies between the tracks, and elements of the tracks, are more clearly visible.

We run two documentation tracks, one for the PPM and another for all of the other documentation that is required. These two tracks are the most interactive and require complete engagement from all parties in order to ensure that each draft is reviewed and revised and re-circulated as quickly and comprehensively as possible.

The third track is the fund incorporation, a fairly standardized process.

The fourth is KYC. This covers everything associated with getting the sponsors approved with all parties. As we explain in Appendix V – KYC and AML, Front Shore's services here are quite unique — we collate all the requirements from every party, consolidate them, and assist with gathering and verification of the documentation and ultimately the distribution and confirmation that all documentation has been received and is satisfactory.

The fifth track is internal account setup, and it is necessary that all of service providers have it in place prior to fund launch.

The sixth track is regulatory approval. This is the key dependent track as we can't approach CIMA until all of the documentation has been finalized, the company has been incorporated, and the KYC is in place.

From start to finish, the whole process can be finalized in as little as 6-8 weeks, but we see launch generally take place between 8 to 14 weeks after initiation of the process, and the project plan below is a consciously un-aggressive plan which illustrates a 14-week project from initiation.

BEFORE WE GET STARTED...

Before starting, there are some key elements of the fund that we need to establish in order to determine our options.

Our imaginary fund is going to be called The Exemplar Fund Ltd (the "Fund"). It is a stand-alone fund with a long-short strategy investing solely in listed equities on established exchanges. It expects to raise approximately $50 million in its first few months and hopes to grow to $200 million within the first two years of operation. It will have monthly subscriptions and redemptions with a minimum investment amount of $500,000. At this point, it will not be taking any U.S. investors.

On that basis, the fund intends to register with CIMA as a Registered Fund.

The Investment Manager to the Fund, Exemplar Manager Ltd, is already registered as an Excluded Person with CIMA under SIBL, and has filed all of the documentation necessary together with Form SIBL(AD) and paid the requisite fees.

ON YOUR MARKS, GET SET...

TRACK 1: PPM
(offering memorandum)

– Your offshore law firm will prepare the first draft of the PPM and circulate it to all parties for review.

– A second draft will be prepared based on the comments received from all parties. Each service provider is responsible for the language that is associated with them in the document, and the Investment Manager is also responsible for all language related to the investment strategy and for ensuring that all risks associated with the strategy are adequately described.

– A third, fourth and probably fifth draft will be prepared and circulated. At this point, Front Shore will assume responsibility for ensuring that all parties contribute to the final document and the offshore law firm will control the changes.

MILESTONE 1:

PPM Finalized

KEY RISK

#1

PPM RISK:
TRACK 1

Any delay in the PPM track will delay the launch of the Fund; the difficulty in this track is getting people to respond in a timely manner.

The best way to avoid any single party holding up the finalization is to define a set amount of time at the outset (3 weeks, we will say) for the entire process, and to re-circulate each draft at agreed-upon points. That way, if a certain party doesn't provide feedback by the deadline, the new draft will still be circulated and their comments will have

to be taken into account in the next draft. There is, however, certain information that must be provided by each party, and if they fail to do this by the final cut-off date, there is no option but to wait; naturally, we take steps to avoid this at all costs.

TRACK 2: OTHER DOCUMENTATION

– Memorandum and Articles of Association (this task appears in track 3 as well, covering the creation of the Fund entity itself)

– First draft circulated for approval.

– Amendments made based on comments received and changes to the terms and conditions of the offering as contained in the PPM.

– Launch Resolution

– First draft circulated for approval, usually only minor comments received.

– By the second or third draft, this document should be finalized and ready for execution upon establishment of the fund.

KEY RISK

#2

THE OTHER DOCUMENTATION

RISK – TRACK 2

The company itself cannot be incorporated until the Memorandum and Articles are finalized,

which usually can't be done until the PPM is close to finalized on, at the very least, the share classes and basic terms of the offering.

SUBSCRIPTION DOCUMENTS:

– Both the onshore and offshore lawyers will draft these documents, with different sets of documents for investors coming from different jurisdictions. U.S. investors, in particular, will have a separate 'sub doc' to non-U.S. investors.

– The administrator will also have substantial input into these documents, as they are usually responsible for KYC and AML procedures for the fund on an ongoing basis and these are detailed in the sub docs.

– Subscription documents can go through five or more iterations prior to finalization, and entirely new documents may be required at a late stage should a new type of investor (either from a different jurisdiction or, perhaps, US tax- exempt) emerge prior to launch.

IMA

– Usually prepared by the investment manager or the onshore law firm.

– The fund's offshore law firm and independent directors for the fund should review this prior to execution and the terms, naturally, need to match the disclosures made in the PPM.

ADMINISTRATION AGREEMENT

– Prepared by the administrator and negotiated with the sponsor on behalf of the fund.

– Again, the fund's offshore law firm and independent directors for the fund should review this prior to execution and the terms must match the PPM.

REGISTERED OFFICE AGREEMENT

– Prepared by the registered office and agent in Cayman, this is a fairly standardized document that will not undergo many changes or drafts.

DIRECTORSHIP AGREEMENT

– Usually prepared by the director, it may also be drafted by the onshore or offshore law firm.

ADMINISTRATIVE CONSENT LETTER

– This is a standard document prepared by the administrator for regulatory purposes.

AUDITOR CONSENT LETTER

– This is also a standard document, prepared by the auditor for regulatory purposes.

MF1 FORM

(This is the appropriate form because we are creating a Registered Fund)

– This form is usually drafted by the offshore law firm, once all of the information required to complete it has been finalized (all parties appointed, terms of the offering settled, directors appointed, and PPM in final form).

TRACK 3: FUND INCORPORATION

– Apply for and reserve name

– Draft Memorandum and Articles of Association (see 2.1 above for more details)

– Incorporation

– Appointment of First Directors

– Issuance of First Shares

– Receipt of Corporate Documentation Pack

– Execute Launch Resolution

MILESTONE 2:

KYC complete

KEY RISK

#3

KYC RISK:

TRACK 4

TRACK 4: KYC

It is hard to exaggerate the potential that this track has to delay launch or derail the entire project.

The KYC track inevitably takes longer, causes more frustration and yields more surprises than any other track. Without completion of this track for each and every party, the Fund cannot launch.

TRACK 5: INTERNAL ACCOUNT SETUP

– Registered Office to set up entity and associated parties within system.

– Administrator to set up fund account within system and confirm completion.

– Prime broker to confirm completion of Fund account setup.

– Bank and Custodian to confirm completion of Fund account setup.

– Auditor to confirm completion of Fund account setup.

TRACK 6: REGULATORY APPROVAL

– Submit all final documentation: MF1, PPM, signed consent letters — to CIMA for registration.

– Receive confirmation of fund registration.

MILESTONE 3:

Fund registered and ready for launch.

In the Front Shore approach to fund setup, we assume responsibility for setting the timetable and responsibilities at the outset, and also for then ensuring that all parties keep to the agreed timetable.

We identify where delays will have a knock-on effect further down the road due to the inherent dependencies in the process, and we finish the process off with a one-week transition process where all documentation and relationships are handed over to the appropriate parties.

We regularly stay on board as consultants to the fund on a retainer basis for the first 12-24 months of the fund's operations, handling any other issues that arise and keeping the fund and investment manager apprised of relevant developments and considerations within the Cayman Islands and the offshore fund industry as a whole.

ALTERNATE RISK

FUND
INCORPORATION

Although this is a well-worn path, there is a risk of delay here,

primarily due to uncertainty around the name or identity of the directors, for example, or the KYC associated with any of the parties involved.

It is imperative to have this structure ready and waiting and able to supply its own KYC to service providers well in advance of the launch date

NEXT PAGE MORE DE-TAILS

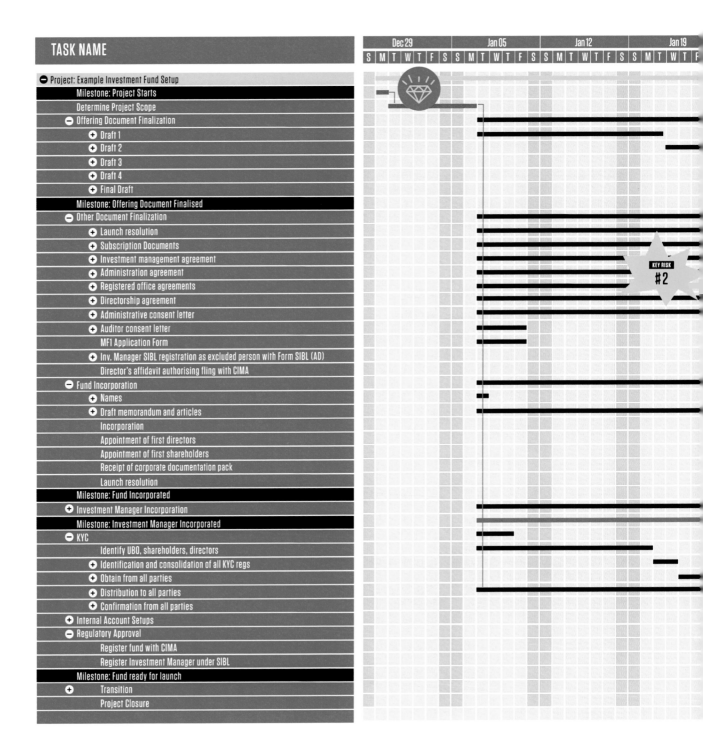

TASK NAME	Dec 29							Jan 05							Jan 12							Jan 19			
	S	M	T	W	T	F	S	S	M	T	W	T	F	S	S	M	T	W	T	F	S	S	M	T	W	T	F
⊖ Project: Example Investment Fund Setup																									
Milestone: Project Starts																									
Determine Project Scope																									
⊖ Offering Document Finalization																									
⊕ Draft 1																									
⊕ Draft 2																									
⊕ Draft 3																									
⊕ Draft 4																									
⊕ Final Draft																									
Milestone: Offering Document Finalised																									
⊖ Other Document Finalization																									
⊕ Launch resolution																									
⊕ Subscription Documents																									
⊕ Investment management agreement																									
⊕ Administration agreement																									
⊕ Registered office agreements																									
⊕ Directorship agreement																									
⊕ Administrative consent letter																									
⊕ Auditor consent letter																									
MF1 Application Form																									
⊕ Inv. Manager SIBL registration as excluded person with Form SIBL (AD)																									
Director's affidavit authorising fling with CIMA																									
⊖ Fund Incorporation																									
⊕ Names																									
⊕ Draft memorandum and articles																									
Incorporation																									
Appointment of first directors																									
Appointment of first shareholders																									
Receipt of corporate documentation pack																									
Launch resolution																									
Milestone: Fund Incorporated																									
⊕ Investment Manager Incorporation																									
Milestone: Investment Manager Incorporated																									
⊖ KYC																									
Identify UBO, shareholders, directors																									
⊕ Identification and consolidation of all KYC regs																									
⊕ Obtain from all parties																									
⊕ Distribution to all parties																									
⊕ Confirmation from all parties																									
⊕ Internal Account Setups																									
⊖ Regulatory Approval																									
Register fund with CIMA																									
Register Investment Manager under SIBL																									
Milestone: Fund ready for launch																									
⊕ Transition																									
Project Closure																									

KEY RISK #2

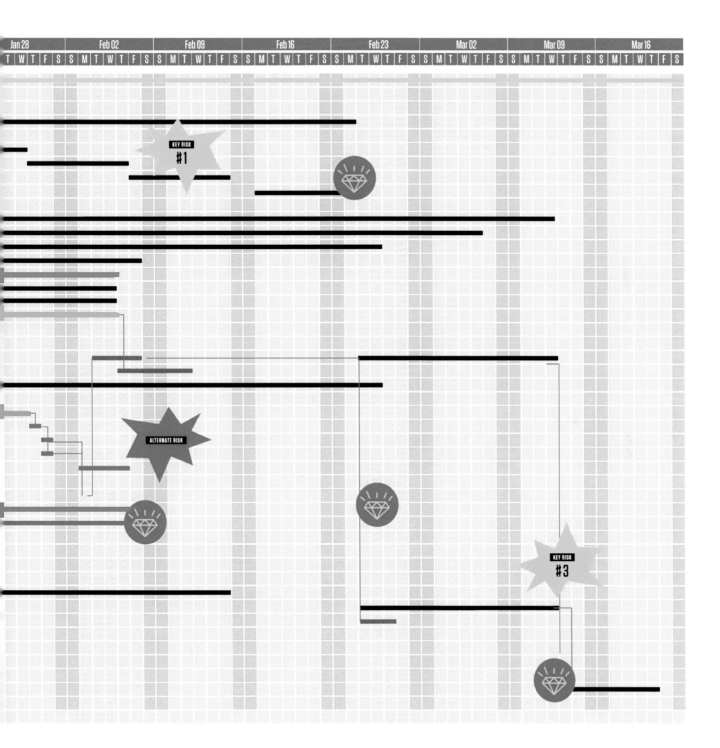

CHAP TER EIGHT

CHAPTER 8
Corporate Governance

Although corporate governance has become both the bane and buzzword of the financial services industry, in its best manifestation it encompasses everything from strategic infrastructures to corporate social responsibility — an honest commitment to all stakeholders, for any corporation is borne of an effective culture of corporate governance — it just doesn't sound very exciting.

I want to highlight three areas of corporate governance that are crucial considerations to the fund from the very beginning. Throughout the life of the fund the hot topics are bound to change and you will need to address your investors' issues and concerns in this regard as and when they arise. But let's start with these three for now:

DIRECTOR'S DUTIES

This issue has always been a big concern of mine as I've been acting as an independent director of a small number of funds since 2005. In my opinion, most lawyers and directors are, and have always been, well aware of their fiduciary obligations as directors, the risks inherent in the role, and the importance of appointing appropriate people to the board.

However, questions around the nature of the services provided by independent directors recently became a topic of conversation due to (1) litigation in Cayman (Weavering Capital) that centered around directors' obligations; (2) the recent increase in attention from the international media on offshore companies and "shell companies" and their "shell directors"; and (3) the fact that CIMA launched an industry consultation process on the issue of directorships at the beginning of 2013. (And has since issued a Statement of Guidance as a result; links are provided in the Appendix and on our website.)

In my opinion, Weavering itself hasn't made any new law, and the draft Statement of Guidance doesn't look to have done much other than summarize some of the law around this topic and make a few recommendations (namely, hold board meetings at least twice a year and keep a register of conflicts of interest).

So let's have a look at the essential duties and best practices of a director of a Cayman fund and any related issues that should be paid special attention to.

A director of any company has two broad duties: a fiduciary duty, and a duty to exercise due skill and care in the performance of their role on the board.

A common misconception is that directors, and the board as a whole, must aim to look after the best interests of the shareholders of the company. In fact, the board must look after the best interests of the company as a whole.

In the context of a normal trading and operating company, the stakeholders will include the shareholders, the employees, and the customers. In certain companies that embrace conscious capitalism or stakeholder theory, the stakeholders to which the board owes an obligation will include the community, the environment, and various other groups and individuals.

In the context of a fund, however, it may actually be more accurate to stress that the primary stakeholders to whom the board owes its fiduciary duty are indeed the shareholders of the fund.

*The fiduciary duty itself can be broken down into the **duty to act in good faith and a duty to avoid and disclose conflicts of interest.***

The Director's duty to exercise due skill and care is traditionally divided into an objective obligation and a subjective obligation.

Under the objective test, the question is whether or not a director is acting with the skill and care that you can expect from somebody holding such a position; in other words, if you're the director of a hedge fund, I'm entitled to assume that you know what a hedge fund is, what the strategy is, and so on.

Under the subjective test, the question is whether or not a director is acting with the skill and care that you can expect from that specific individual within that role; in other words, if the director happens to be a retired judge, you are entitled to expect her to have more knowledge and experience in the legal issues facing the fund than you would from a director with no legal experience or knowledge.

Beyond those duties, there are some specific issues under Cayman law that deserve mentioning.

The Directors are ultimately responsible for all of the following:

MUST ENSURE THAT PROPER RECORDS ARE KEPT, INCLUDING REGISTERS AND ACCOUNTS;

REPORTING OBLIGATIONS (TO THE REGISTRAR, TO CIMA) MUST BE COMPLIED WITH;

ASSETS IN SEGREGATED PORTFOLIO COMPANIES MUST BE KEPT SEPARATE;

ANTI-MONEY LAUNDERING OBLIGATIONS MUST BE COMPLIED WITH.

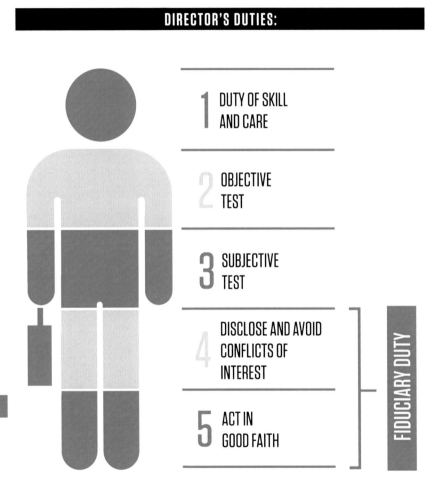

DIRECTOR'S DUTIES:

1 DUTY OF SKILL AND CARE

2 OBJECTIVE TEST

3 SUBJECTIVE TEST

4 DISCLOSE AND AVOID CONFLICTS OF INTEREST

5 ACT IN GOOD FAITH

FIDUCIARY DUTY

SHADOW DIRECTORS:

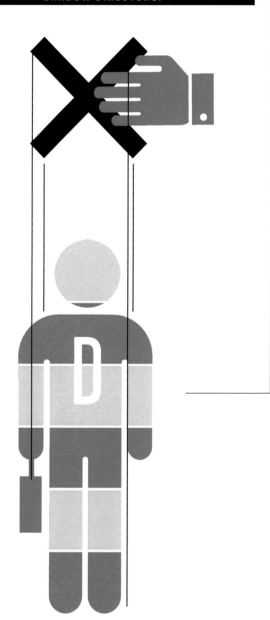

A "shadow director" is a puppet master. Defined under UK law as a "person in accordance with whose direction or instructions the directors of a company are accustomed to act."

The problem is that if a shadow director exercises near-total control over the board, that person will be treated under the law as if they were an actual director, so liability and obligations that might apply to the board would apply to them, too, potentially including the obligation to disclose conflicts of interest, or beneficial interests.

It is not hard to imagine a scenario where the sponsor or investment manager of the fund would be deemed a Shadow Director.

Directors of funds are, with very few exceptions, not involved in making any investment decisions, they are almost always non-executive directors. The investment decisions of the fund are delegated, via contract, to the investment manager of the fund.

The board retains an obligation to ensure that the manager is acting in compliance with the Investment Management Agreement and any restrictions contained in the PPM, but they are not expected, nor is it appropriate for them, to monitor or opine on the day-to-day trading activities of the fund.

DIRECTOR REGULATION

As we were wrapping things up with the book, Cayman presented legislation (the Directors Registration and Licensing Bill) to authorize CIMA to regulate directors of funds. The regulations themselves are still pending so certain details are not yet known, but the broad strokes are pretty clear.

Going forward, all directors (whether Cayman-based or not) of a fund that is registered with CIMA, or of a Cayman-based investment manager that is registered as an excluded manager under SIBL, will need to be registered with and possibly licensed by CIMA.

If the director is an individual with less than 20 fund directorships, then he or she will have to simply register with CIMA, and pay application and annual fees of USD 853.66.

If an individual has more than 20 directorships she is a "Professional Director" and will have to pay USD 3,658.54 annually, and if the director

is a corporate entity then it is a "Corporate Director" and the annual fees due are USD 9,756.10. Both Professional and Corporate directors have to apply for an actual license from CIMA. In this case, CIMA will apply a test to determine if the applicant is fit and proper prior to granting the license.

There are a few exceptions to the licensing rules for directors that are part of an entity that is already licensed in Cayman or by the SEC or the FCA and so on.

RISK MANAGEMENT

While the investment manager usually does a very good and comprehensive job of identifying the key risks inherent within the investment strategy, less attention tends to be focused on the general risk management approach of the fund as an enterprise in and of itself.

Key risks that are applicable to the fund should all be identified and discussed by the board of the fund at their regular board meetings. The primary categories to be examined are the fund structure, the regulatory and compliance environment both locally and globally, counterparty risk, liquidity, internal controls, leverage, key man issues, insurance, and the risks inherent within the investment strategy.

SHAREHOLDER TREATMENT

One of the key principles of corporate law is that shareholders in a particular class are treated fairly; accordingly, a frequently asked question is whether or not any particular action taken by the fund by the board of directors treats one or more of the shareholders prejudicially.

In most cases it's possible to empower the board of directors with sufficient discretion to waive certain requirements and procedures (such as notice periods as they relate to redemptions or subscriptions) such that treating one shareholder favorably will not be seen as prejudicial to the others.

But it's a different story in the event that lock-up periods or redemption suspensions are introduced in a situation where there was no precedent for it established in the PPM or other documentation.

As you will see in the chapter on side letters, those documents can also be deemed to be prejudicial to those shareholders that are not a party to the side letter.

So what is the lesson to be learned from all of this? A good offshore lawyer will ensure that all of these situations are raised with the fund sponsor during the process of drafting the PPM, and that appropriate language is inserted into the document to ensure that there is sufficient flexibility granted to the fund.

For example, a clause stating that under certain circumstances redemptions will be suspended indefinitely might seem outrageous at the time the fund is launched, but it could be the only thing that saves the fund when the fan gets hit.

The important thing is to go through the mental exercise of thinking all of these issues through and making an informed decision about what to include and what to exclude.

The basic issues are as follows, but it's really very important to speak to your offshore counsel about this prior to finalizing the PPM: ability to enter into side letters, suspension of redemptions, waiver of notice periods, waiver of minimum investment amounts, ability to pay out redemptions in kind, ability to pay out partial redemptions, ability to hold back a portion of redemptions, and ability to suspend payment of final redemption amount.

WE'VE PUT A CHECKLIST UP ON

(WWW. GORDONCASEY.COM)

under the Resources section – please go there and download for your own fund.

CHAP TER NINE

CHAPTER 9
Different Legal Entities

As outlined in the introduction, we have explained and will continue to analyze, companies throughout this guide, and all illustrations and details are written on the assumption that the fund has been structured as a company.

While this is indeed the most common form of fund entity in Cayman, it is not the only kind available. I would like to give some essential details on the other legal entities that are available for funds in the Caymans. The one exception is Segregated Portfolio Companies, which I talk about in sufficient detail in Chapter Ten – Fund Structure, as they constitute a distinct structure both in terms of their corporate essence, and in terms of how the fund's investments are arranged.

SEGREGATED PORTFOLIO COMPANIES

UNIT TRUSTS

A Trust is a contractual arrangement that is created by a Trust Deed. Unlike companies, trusts don't have legal personality, so they can't waltz around entering into contracts on their own behalf — they rely on the trustee to perform that function for them.

Unit trusts issue units to investors, and each unit represents a beneficial interest in the assets of the trust (which

assets are being held by the trustee, on behalf of the trust). There are legal niceties at play here which may be of interest to you: the investors are not co-owners of the trust or the assets of the trust — they just have this beneficial interest and, typically, it amounts specifically to the right to exchange their units for their cash value (i.e. Redeem them at the then-current NAV.).

Unit trusts are very popular in Japan where they are the most common form of investment vehicle locally and may have preferential tax treatment as well.

Cayman also offers something called a STAR trust, which, amongst other things, allows for the appointment of an Enforcer, whose role it is to enforce the rights of beneficiaries.

LIMITED PARTNERSHIPS

Limited Partnerships (LP), like companies and unlike regular partnerships, limit the liability of the partners to the contribution that they make to the LP.

Each LP needs to have a General Partner who more or less functions as the management arm of the LP, similar to the board of directors of a company or the trustee of a trust, although, naturally, there are unique, technical legal distinctions amongst all of these roles. But they also lack legal personality in the strict sense and the General Partner (GP) usually enters into contracts on their behalf.

LP's are created in Cayman by drafting up a partnership agreement and then registering the LP with the Registrar.

Partners are issued partnership interests and a register is kept similar to a shareholder register. Partners actually do become joint owners of the assets of the partnership, although for practical purposes they function the same way as other funds in terms of subscriptions and redemptions and NAV's.

The General Partner is frequently, although not always, also the investment manager to the fund. The fund documentation will make this clear, together with which activities and duties have been delegated to the GP and which to the manager, if they are separate parties.

CHAP
TER
TEN

CHAPTER 10
Fund Structures

In all likelihood you are already quite familiar with the options available to you when structuring your fund. However, this is not common knowledge outside of the industry and it may be beneficial to see some illustrations of both the simple form of such structures, as well as the more complicated (looking) combinations of structures that are out there.

In this chapter we're going to have a look at stand-alone funds, master-feeders, fund-of-funds, segregated portfolio companies, and side-by-side structures. The idea is to give a brief description of each with a suggestion regarding the reasoning that might underlie such a structure and then to illustrate the idea with a pretty little diagram.

STAND-ALONE FUNDS

The simplest of all structures, this is one fund, with one set of investors, making investments directly.

MASTER-FEEDER STRUCTURES

Probably the most common structure after a stand-alone fund, is the master-feeder structure. The essential idea is that you have an onshore fund and an offshore fund (the "Feeder funds"). Each of these funds is available for those investors for whom the specific fund makes the most sense from a tax and regulatory point of view; those two funds subsequently invest all of their money into the master fund, which then makes the actual investments in accordance with the investment strategy.

FUND-OF-FUNDS

Starting in the early 1980s, investors started to have the option of investing into multiple funds and thereby achieving a level of hedge fund diversification usually only available to much wealthier investors, by investing in a single fund that would then place investments into the other funds.

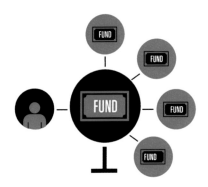

These "funds-of-funds" are very attractive for obvious reasons and soon grew substantially in popularity across the globe. They are very interesting beasts, as they are similar to funds in a lot of ways but they are also different, in that, of course, investors, sitting on both sides of the fence as they do, are in a unique position in relation to the funds in which they invest. It is likely that it is the investigative and quality assurance work performed by funds-of-funds, more than the basic due diligence performed by other large investors, that gave way to the operational due diligence procedures that are now quite commonplace, and growing, throughout the industry.

Structurally speaking, however, there is little to distinguish a fund-of-funds from another fund, and they may be structured along any of the same categories as a traditional fund.

The only real difference is in the target investment, so in this sense they can be considered more as a distinct strategy than a distinct structure. But they are a unique form of fund, to my mind, and this seemed the most appropriate place to introduce them. On this page is a simple fund-of-funds structure with investments into four different funds (which would be an unusually small number for most funds-of-funds). As mentioned above, however, it could just as easily be structured as a stand-alone fund, or as a side-by-side structure.

allows separate investments while protecting each class, or portfolio, from the liabilities of the other portfolios within the fund.

UMBRELLA FUNDS

An umbrella fund is one that operates multiple strategies, or separate investment pools, "under one umbrella." Investors into a typical umbrella fund might, for example, subscribe for Class A shares, knowing that Class A shares will only participate in investments into bonds. Or they might subscribe for some Class A, and some Class C, adding some listed equities to their investment.

These days, the most common structure used for an umbrella fund is the Segregated Portfolio Company (see below). A traditional fund carries the risk that while an investor may have only subscribed for Class A shares, the Class X shares incurred a huge liability which wiped out the whole fund, Class A included. A Segregated Portfolio Company

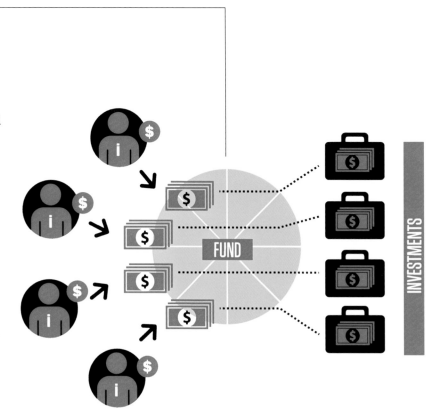

SEGREGATED PORTFOLIO COMPANIES

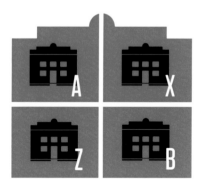

This is a relatively new innovation in company law — a form of limited liability company in which the company is able to create cells, or portfolios, within itself, and each such cell is a separate entity insofar as obligations and liabilities are concerned.

The effect is to ensure that there is no cross-liability between the cells, effectively enabling a single legal entity to have multiple ring-fenced assets, each with limited liability; the equivalent of having multiple corporate entities without the added regulatory burden of multiple corporate entities. (See the section on Umbrella Funds above as well.)

Segregated Portfolio Companies (SPCs) or a legally equivalent structure, originated in Guernsey and Delaware and are currently available in at least 13 countries or states, including Anguilla, Bermuda, BVI, Guernsey, Ireland, Isle of Man, Jersey, Malta, Mauritius, and Qatar. In Cayman, they been available since 1998 (exclusively for insurance companies) and were permitted for other companies in 2012. In BVI, they were authorized for fund structures while I was writing this book (in late 2013) and legislation to allow them is on the table in a number of other jurisdictions.

As you can imagine, it is possible to effectively run a number of funds with completely different strategies and investments via an SPC while only having a single corporate entity, service providers and board of directors.

Although it is possible to create a separate PPM for each portfolio, a common practice is to have an over-arching PPM for the entire SPC, and an additional term sheet or supplement for each portfolio. Both the PPM and the term sheet must be registered with CIMA prior to launch.

It goes without saying (almost), but it is clearly far easier to launch a new fund when all that is required is the creation of a new portfolio and a supplement to the PPM detailing the terms of that particular offering.

The creation of a portfolio can be done via resolution if the Articles stipulate that, and if there is no requirement to file any amendments or notices with the Registrar in order for the new portfolio to be effective. There is, however, an extra fee associated with each additional portfolio; your registered office will be able to draft the resolution and ensure that the requisite fees are paid in a timely manner.

In any event, a common structure is to have two funds running side-by-side, making the same investments. In all likelihood they will not be able to obtain the exact same price for the investments they make, and the offering documentation will usually mention that as a risk factor together with a disclaimer around it.

SIDE BY SIDE FUNDS

Again, investors from different parts of the world are going to ask to have an option for investing that makes sense from a tax point of view. It may be the case that consolidating the funds from onshore and offshore investors into a master fund has a trickle-down negative affect on certain investors; or you may have been operating the onshore fund for years and to move to a master fund just doesn't make any practical sense.

CHAP
TER
ELEVEN

CHAPTER 11
Operational Due Diligence

There is a growing, and admirable, trend for large, usually institutional, investors to engage independent consultants to perform a due diligence review on a fund that they are considering. These consultants will usually visit the fund manager's office, spend time with them, and, as you would expect, ask a lot of questions.

I believe that this industry has blossomed recently due to a combination of the abundance of talent and experience within the fund industry itself and the corporate scandals of the past decade or so — a number of which have been related, if somewhat tangentially, to the hedge fund industry. Additionally, a large number of funds locked in their investors and suspended redemptions at the height of the financial crisis, and this exposed operational risks that investors had not considered before, so, "once bitten…" etc.

While Front Shore does not perform this service, we admire those that do, and we feel that all new funds should start thinking how they will approach Operational Due Diligence (ODD) reviews and should immediately begin to prepare the documentation to demonstrate to such consultants that they share the concerns of their investors, and that they recognize the value of the procedures and processes that they are frequently looking for.

In reality, of course, whether or not one of these consultants ever turns up on your doorstep is irrelevant; while they may technically only represent one or two investors, the process is representative of the concerns of all potential investors, so preparation will certainly not be time wasted.

The primary, *sine qua non,* **goal of the operational due diligence consultant is to ensure that there are sufficient accounting controls and procedures in place, and that the legal terms and conditions of the operation are documented. But that really is just the very beginning.**

Beyond that, they are looking for a fund that is run as any good business would be: a culture that matches the fund's stated goals, particularly in regard to risk appetite in relation to investments; an operational philosophy over and above an investment philosophy; sufficient investment in infrastructure, training and staff to ensure that the business is capable of running smoothly and capturing value as intended; segregation of duties and tools to manage conflicts of interest; general workflow and process

documentation; and some system to ensure that the ever-changing legal and regulatory environment is monitored and complied with.

And of course, they're always on the lookout for the next Bernie Madoff.

In all likelihood, the investment manager and their service providers will receive an extensive due diligence questionnaire (DDQ). These may be extremely laborious to complete, but it is a healthy process and there may be opportunities to improve hidden within the questions.

I have heard, on more than one occasion, that the best managers seek out feedback on how they can improve and view the ODD process as a chance to get valuable advice (while it is being paid for by the investor).

Bear in mind, as well, that if the investor does make an investment, you are probably going to be getting regular visits as a "health check" from time to time. And if you don't receive that investment, you

should definitely ask for some feedback on why and see if you can improve your systems, processes and approach to the ODD visit before the next consultant shows up.

CHAP TER TWELVE

CHAPTER 12
Side Pockets

Things don't always go the way we plan. Illiquid investments, or investments that turn illiquid, cause a bit of a conundrum for a fund with investors coming in and out at regular intervals.

Imagine a fund with 4 investors. At the beginning, all is going well and you could say that each investor owns 25% of the fund.

For argument's sake, imagine that 2 of the investors redeem all of their shares and, in order to pay them out, the fund has to sell off some of the investments; they do so and things are fine, except that while they were deciding which of the investments to sell in order to raise the cash to pay out the redemptions, they noticed that some of their investments, accounting for 20% of their funds, didn't have a market and was pretty much illiquid. They carried on, however, but now that investment constitutes 40% of the remaining value in the fund. What to do?

If they do nothing, and all of the investors keep redeeming in turn, for whatever reason, you will end up with 1 investor whose entire investment is 80% illiquid and 20% liquid.

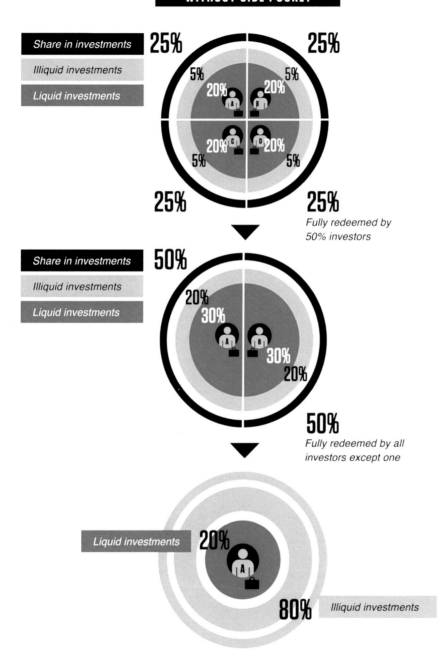

WITHOUT SIDE POCKET

Share in investments
Illiquid investments
Liquid investments

25%   25%
5%   5%
20%   20%
20%   20%
5%   5%
25%   25%

Fully redeemed by 50% investors

Share in investments
Illiquid investments
Liquid investments

50%
20%
30%
30%
20%
50%

Fully redeemed by all investors except one

Liquid investments   20%
80%   Illiquid investments

SIDE POCKETS

So here comes the Side Pocket. The idea here is that illiquid investments are separated from the rest of the fund's assets and investors holding shares in the fund at the time that the assets are "side pocketed" will exchange an appropriate number of normal shares (let's call them Class A) for shares in the class that now holds the side pocket assets (let's call it Class SP).

The Class SP shares can't be redeemed or subscribed for separately; they are initially a direct function of your investment in Class A shares at the time that the assets are determined to be illiquid, and they are subsequently a function of the assets being liquidated over time.

Liquid investments

5% 20% A 20% 5%

Illiquid investments

5% 5%
5% 5%

Redemption by 50% of investors

Liquid investments

40% A D 40%

A B
5% 5%
5% 5%
C D

20%

Illiquid Investments in Side Pockets

Redemption by all investors except one

Liquid investments

80% A

A B
5% 5%
5% 5%
C D

20%

Illiquid Investments in Side Pockets

As the assets are liquidated, the proceeds attributable to each investor in accordance with the number and percentage of Class SP shares they hold will be paid out to those investors who have fully redeemed their Class A Shares, and will be re-subscribed, at the then-current NAV, into Class A for those shareholders who are still current investors in the fund. And shareholders who have partially redeemed from Class A subsequent to the creation of the Class SP shares will receive a partial pay out and a partial re-subscription into Class A.

As you can see from the illustration, the result of redemptions where a side pocket is employed is ultimately that nobody ever owns more than their fair share of illiquid investments, but investors that wish to redeem will not get a full redemption until the illiquid portions have been sold off.

CHAP TER THIR TEEN

CHAPTER 13
Listing

There are a number of investors who are only permitted to invest in funds listed on a recognized stock exchange. The key reason for funds seeking to list on an exchange is in order to gain access to such investors; it may offer tax advantages to certain investors and, as you will recall, it will also enable the fund to be registered as a Listed Fund

There are many choices for listing funds, including Ireland, Luxembourg, Toronto, AIM in London and the Dutch Caribbean Securities Exchange in Curacao. The listing regime in Cayman is by far one of the most popular for offshore funds.

The Cayman Stock Exchange (CSX) can list bonds, equities and funds, but is primarily a platform for funds, with over 2,000 listings as of 2013. It was launched in 1997 and is regulated by the Stock Exchange Authority in Cayman.

In terms of its international memberships and recognition, it is an affiliated member of IOSCO, the only offshore member of the Intermarket Surveillance Group, an affiliate member of the World Federation of Exchanges and a "recognized stock exchange" with "qualifying investments," according to HMRC in the UK.

From a fund point of view, the applicable Listing Rules and Model Codes of Conduct (see the links in the Appendix and on our website) are intended to be as efficient as possible, meaning that they are simple but effective. In a similar manner to the Irish Stock Exchange, they provide initial comments on listing documents within five days and are committed to a document turnaround time of three days for subsequent drafts.

The essential process is outlined below and can be completed within six weeks after the submission of the first draft of the listing Prospectus:

APPOINT A LISTING AGENT IN CAYMAN

frequently a law firm, or affiliated entity, the agent will be responsible for all dealings with the CSX.

▼

SATISFY THE CSX CONDITIONS FOR LISTING

the essential conditions are detailed in the Listing Rules and we've put a few of them in a box on this page.

PREPARE LISTING DOCUMENTS

the Prospectus must be prepared in accordance with the Listing Rules. The preparation and finalization of this document is likely to take the most time.

▼

APPROVAL

once the Prospectus is approved, it is sent to the Listing Committee for final approval, after which all of the supporting documentation will need to be filed together with the appropriate fees.

▼

LISTING

the technical process of actually listing the fund will then take place, with Bloomberg tickers and so on being captured on the CSX system and Bloomberg, along with marketing materials on the CSX website.

ESSENTIAL CONDITIONS FOR LISTING:

The fund must be domiciled in an approved jurisdiction; it must appoint an auditor within the Cayman Islands; the directors must be approved, have adequate experience and expertise and take individual responsibility for the statements in the Prospectus; the investment manager must have appropriate experience and expertise; the fund must appoint a custodian that is a separate entity from the fund's other service providers, with good reputation and possess sufficient experience to fulfill its role; all service providers must disclose any conflicts of interest; securities must be freely transferable; and financial statements must be prepared in accordance with IFRS, UK GAAP or US GAAP.

CONTINUING OBLIGATIONS:

The Model Code is very helpful in laying out best practices expected of the fund's directors and the investment manager and employees, and a lot of the behavior described in there constitutes a continuing obligation, in a sense.

Beyond that, the fund should notify the CSX as soon as possible of any price-sensitive information, material developments and material changes in performance or financial position. NAV's and regular accounts should, obviously, be sent to the CSX immediately, and the primary ongoing obligation is to ensure that all shareholders of a given security are treated equally.

CHAP TER FOUR TEEN

CHAPTER 14
Side Letters

There comes a time in a fund's life when that one special investor comes along and makes everything alright. At first it seems like a match made in hedge heaven, but at some point you realize "he doesn't love me for who I am, he wants to change me". And then, out comes the side letter...

A side letter is a collection of terms and conditions that override the terms and conditions contained in the PPM and the subscription document and possibly even the Memorandum and Articles (rendering the side letter ineffective for the most part, unenforceable in law but pregnant with practical consequences — we'll come to that later).

The philosophy is that the investor, in return for the substantial investment being made, wants, or requires, certain additional conditions to cover their investment into the fund. As you'll recall from Chapter Nine – Corporate Governance, however, preferential treatment of shareholders is a big no-no, so there is a rather large question mark relating to how you enter into a side letter without treating non-side-lettered shareholders in a prejudicial manner.

If you suspect that there are side letters in the future of your fund, you should disclose that in your PPM from day one. The wording should essentially amount to an acknowledgement from the investor that other shareholders may, in effect, be treated preferentially under certain limited conditions based on separate terms and conditions that they may agree to with the fund.

The subscription document should mention it, too. As the details can get a bit complex and it affects a number of different elements of the offering (subscription, transfer, redemption, share classes and board authority and mandate) you'll have to rely heavily on your offshore law firm to get this one right.

Without really going into the arguments here, I would like to point out that while side letters are a practical reality, from a legal point of view there is still an issue. We have no real consensus on whether a disclosure in the PPM and Subscription Documents is a sufficient answer to the question of whether a director who has entered into a side letter has really acted in the best interests of the fund.

(In other words, to harken back to Chapter Eight again, the disclosure may partially answer the preferential treatment issue by obtaining consent, but that does not, in and of itself, mean that the director has discharged his/her fiduciary duty to the fund, nor does it mean that he/she has not.)

In all likelihood it will depend on the specific circumstances surrounding each side letter, as well as how the terms of that side letter are executed should that ultimately be required.

We have described some of the standard terms and conditions that are included in side letters on the opposite page. As you will see, some of these are fairly innocuous, while others can cause quite serious issues, and, indeed, there were many funds that found themselves in a tough position during the recent financial crisis as investors pulled money out of their funds and invoked some of the terms of their side letters, leaving the remaining investors locked into funds that no longer had the liquidity to pay out redemption requests received in the normal course of business.

We note that some terms are unenforceable (those that contradict the Memorandum and Articles of the fund, for example), but being unenforceable does not mean that the investor can't launch litigation against the fund and/or the investment manager for entering in the side letter and accepting the investment; and if the fund acts on the letter despite the term being unenforceable, fund owners may find that the other investors have suffered a loss, and those investors might sue the fund and the investment manager and might hold the directors personally liable for failing to exercise their fiduciary duty both at the time of entering into the letter and when they acted on it.

MOST FAVORED NATION

This is a clause that states that this investor has the best terms of any investor in the fund, and if any other investor gets better terms, then they will get them, too.

FEES

The investor pays different management and performance fees to the rest of the shareholders. This would usually be a fairly clear instance of preferential treatment, but that can be avoided by the fund paying the manager its standard fees and the investment manager then providing the investor with a rebate to the extent laid out in the side letter. Another alternative very commonly used is to create a separate class of shares for the investor.

LIQUIDITY:

There are a whole range of clauses that fall under this heading, but the idea is generally that there will be no liquidity restrictions on the investor, that they will have advance notice and the ability to redeem under certain conditions (key man issues, large redemptions by other investors, redemption by the principal, a specified percentage drop in NAV, investigation

of the fund or investment manager), no payments in kind, no lock-ups, no redemption notification period, and so on. As you will probably have realized as you read that list, most of these are unenforceable (due to the prejudicial effect they will have on other investors).

GRANDFATHERING

This is essentially a statement that no future changes to the terms and conditions of the offering will apply to this investor. Naturally it will be unenforceable to a certain extent (depending on the changes that are made in the future). This clause usually includes a statement that the investor does not give "implied consent" to any changes either.]

One of the mistakes that has made in the past is that the wrong parties enter into the side letter. Either the investment manager has entered into the side letter with the investor and not the fund, or the beneficial owner (rather than the investor of record) has negotiated and signed the document. There are certain elements of the side letter that apply to the manager, but most of them will apply to the fund and, unsurprisingly, while the investment manager has authority to enter into investments on behalf of the fund, they have no authority to enter into legally binding contracts that alter the terms of the fund's offering.

So any side letter that is not signed by the actual investor of record and counter-signed by the fund's actual representative is not a binding agreement.

A very practical issue surrounding side letter is keeping track of them. Success may bring institutional money to your door, and that will likely mean a large number of side letters. Although some of the terms may be similar, certain investors have some very specific requirements and it is an open question as to who will monitor all of the requirements collectively and ensure that they are complied with. It is

likely to be a combination of the investment manager and the administrator, but that will need to be spelled out clearly and may involve a fee increase. And, in the absence of delegation, the obligation will fall directly on the directors of the fund — another reason to exercise caution when entering into side letters.

CHAP TER FIF TEEN

CHAPTER 15
FATCA

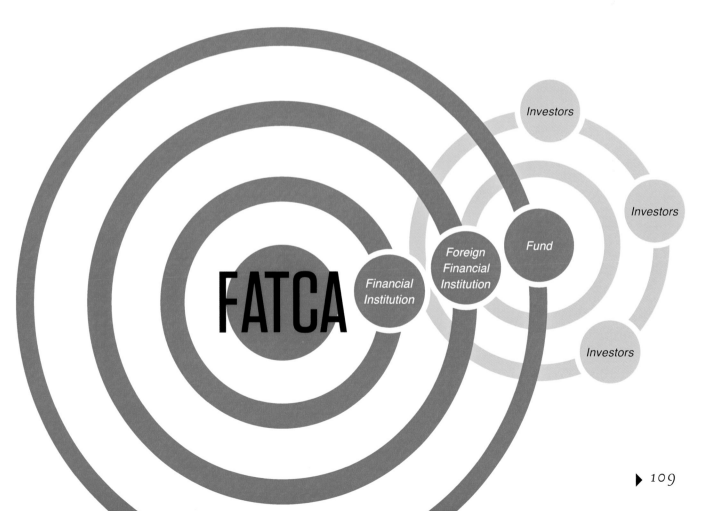

THE BASICS

The Foreign Account Tax Compliance Act, or FATCA, was passed in the U.S. as part of the HIRE Act in 2010 and, despite quite a few delays, is currently effective in regards to certain obligations that it imposes on foreign banks and financial institutions.

Essentially, FATCA says that a foreign financial institution (FFI) must register with the IRS and provide the IRS with certain key information at certain key dates. They are primarily looking for accounts held by "U.S. Persons" in those FFI's.

"But wait," you say, "I don't have any U.S. investors!" Or "I don't have any U.S. investments! I don't deserve to be treated like this."

To quote Clint Eastwood's character in Unforgiven, "Deserve's got nothing to do with it…" FATCA still applies to you, and you need to comply with it one way or another.

FFI's that do not register or otherwise fail to comply with their obligations under FATCA will be subject to a 30 percent withholding on any U.S.-source income sent to that FFI, irrespective of the reason for the transfer.

(At this point let me just bite my tongue and say nothing more than the fact that we will not be discussing the philosophical or ethical (or even legal) implications of a statute that does, or tries to do, something like this. Instead, we will move on…)

INITIAL EFFECT

Above and beyond the extremely basic summary of the most elementary characteristics of FATCA, what does this mean for your Cayman fund? This places three new obligations on the fund that weren't there before:

- Financial institutions that the fund deals with are going to be looking for assurances that the fund is FATCA-compliant, including the number and details of any U.S. Persons involved with the fund in any form (either as investor or, for example, as signatory or authorized person on any accounts held by the fund anywhere).

- You, the fund operator, are going to be asking your own investors to provide assurance to the fund that they are FATCA-compliant, and you will also be asking if there are any U.S. Persons associated with the investor in any way.

- And, perhaps most importantly, the fund needs to ensure that it is FATCA-compliant itself, that it knows whether or not it is a Foreign Financial Institution, a participating FFI, a deemed-compliant FFI, a registered deemed-compliant FFI, a Qualified Collective Investment Vehicle, a restricted fund, a Non-Financial Foreign Entity, or a member of an Expanded Affiliate Group.

And it will also be necessary (in the course of asking those questions) to ask whether any of the people working with or for the fund, or the manager, or the administrator, meet the definition of a U.S. Person (it's more complicated than you think), what sort of FATCA entity they are, and so on.

Clearly it's time to get some legal advice once you get to this point, particularly when you take into account the fact that Cayman signed an Inter-governmental Agreement with the U.S. towards the end of 2013 (the type known as a Model 1 agreement) that shifts some of the reporting burden from the FFI itself to CIMA.

All FFI's still need to register with the IRS on the FATCA portal and get a Global Intermediary Identification Number (GIIN), but some of the reporting will now be made locally, to CIMA, who will then consolidate it and pass it on to the IRS.

SOME STEPS

So now that I haven't cleared up anything, let's have a look at the procedure that you would need to go through at a macro level:

DETERMINE YOUR OBLIGATIONS:

This is currently the most opaque part of the process and there is still no clarity, or common practice, with regards to Cayman funds, managers or other investment entities. While it is fairly clear that both funds and managers will meet the definition of an FFI, it is unclear whether they will be able to take advantage of some of the reduced reporting requirements available to one or more of the forms of deemed-compliant FFI's.

If you have more than one entity in your structure, you will need to look at all of the entities, the fund, the investment manager, any portfolio holding companies, any other entities whatsoever. It is possible that all of them fall under common control and may therefore be part of an Expanded Affiliate Group, which would make reporting a little more efficient as there is some consolidation possible as a result.

MAKE THE NECESSARY REGISTRATIONS

Once you have identified your FFI's, and determined how they should be registered, you will need to go to the IRS website (see the link in the Resources section and on our website) and register your FFI or register your FFI's as a group if they are part of an Expanded Affiliate Group. After you have registered, you will be issued a GIIN.

Even though Cayman's IGA will be in force, you will need to obtain your GIIN in order to comply with the local requirements that will be implemented in order for Cayman to comply with its obligations under the IGA.

Technically speaking, under a Model 1 IGA, FFI's which register with the IRS do so only to obtain their GIIN, and they do not agree to the FFI agreement on the site (otherwise they would have duplicate obligations to comply directly to the IRS and to CIMA in Cayman).

COMPLY
(due diligence and reporting)

Now that you've got your GIIN and you're bound to comply with FATCA either directly or via CIMA and the local Cayman reporting obligations, you need to start the process of compliance. It's likely that your independent fund administrator will do most of the heavy lifting here, but you should understand the basic requirements, as they will likely cause some friction with your investors.

Existing investors who hold less than $1 million get a slight pass, as the obligation here is for you to review your electronic records and look for "U.S.

indicia"; you know, things like a U.S. address, a U.S. passport, a U.S. bank account, and so on. If you find them, then you need to dig a little deeper and try to find out if the investor is a U.S. Person.

New investors will need to certify that they are not a U.S. Person, and their certification should match up with the other KYC docs that they provide.

Anybody who is a U.S. Person will need to send you their Tax Identification Number (TIN).

Once you have all of that done, the reporting obligations will essentially amount to submitting that information (name, TIN) together with their balance at the end of the year and (once later reporting obligations kick in) interest, dividends, other income, and gross proceeds.

TIMELINE

As I mentioned earlier, FATCA's implementation has been subject to a number of delays, so any timelines that you see

should be taken with a pinch of salt, and you should also check the publication date to make sure it hasn't been superseded. KPMG and EY both have fantastic FATCA resources and there is a link to their pages in Appendix II – Resources, and on www.gordoncasey.com.

> *KPMG and EY both have fantastic FATCA resources;*
>
> ## THERE IS A LINK TO THEIR PAGES IN APPENDIX II – RESOURCES, AND ON
>
> (WWW. GORDONCASEY.COM)

CHAP TER SIX TEEN

CHAPTER 16
AIFMD

WHAT'S IN A NAME?

One of the main differences between U.S. legislation and European legislation is that the Europeans don't care if you can't pronounce the acronym for their legislation. Try saying AIFMD 20 times at a cocktail party and you may stop mocking the effort that went into naming the JOBS Act, the HIRE Act, or even FATCA for that matter — in case you haven't noticed, FATCA is just one letter away from FatCat; this is not a coincidence.

The Alternative Investment Fund Managers Directive ("AIFMD" or the "Directive") was enacted with the goal of creating a uniform set of standards for funds that are marketed across Europe —

the idea being, essentially, that an investor in Germany, for example, should be able to assume that the same fundamental level of regulatory oversight is applicable to any European manager she invests with, as would be the case for any German manager she invests with.

Again, I'm going to resist the temptation to delve into the politics of the legislation. It is active and in force as of 22 July 2013 and some member states, but not all, have successfully transposed the directive into local law (they were supposed to all have had this wrapped up by 22 July 2013).

But what does it all mean for Cayman Funds? Well, basically, if you are marketing your fund within the European Union (EU), or to EU investors, you have to comply with the Directive. You may continue to market to professional investors under the national private placement regimes currently in place, provided that you comply with some of the basic AIFMD requirements regarding

annual reports, disclosure to investors and reporting obligations; and provided that there is a co-operation agreement (a Memorandum of Understanding) between the EU jurisdiction where you are active and your non-EU jurisdiction (for our purposes, Cayman — and yes, there are 27 MoU's in place, out of a possible 31 – Slovenia and Croatia don't seem to be signing any!) and that your domicile is not listed as non-cooperative on the Financial Action Task Force (FATF) list (Cayman is not, of course). These national private placement regimes are being phased out by 2018, though.

Beyond that, in due course (2015), it will be possible for non-EU managers and non-EU funds to take advantage of the "passporting" scheme within the EU, so that the fund may be marketed across Europe, but you will have to be in full compliance with AIFMD.

It's worth mentioning that funds which do not market in the EU at all are not subject to the requirements of the directive. There are two noteworthy approaches that take advantage of that: the first is that there are marketing agencies that are fully compliant with the AIFMD that can take on that role for you, and the second is that you can accept EU investors that approach you — the so-called reverse solicitation exemption.

This is, as you can see, a very recent development (at least in terms of its operation in practice) and the experts are still ironing out some of the details. We are seeing some rather divergent opinions on what is required structurally for new funds in order to be in compliance. We strongly recommend consulting with your offshore law firm in order to obtain the latest advice on how to structure the fund for your specific needs in relation to EU investors. Cayman, as a whole, is at the forefront of the charge in obtaining cooperation agreements, and Cayman law firms have the most experience in structuring offshore funds to best comply with AIFMD.

2018 is the year by which the AIFMD will have replaced all of the private placement regimes in each jurisdiction and will be, in effect, fully operational. Until then, there are various elements being implemented and transposed in each jurisdiction.

CHAPTER SEVEN TEEN

CHAPTER 17
ERISA

The Employee Retirement Income Security Act (ERISA) is a very large, complex and comprehensive piece of legislation. The part that concerns us is the part that defines which investment funds fall under the scope of the law, and the consequences to that fund in terms of governance, regulation, and restrictions.

Essentially, in the event that more than 25 percent of a given fund's investors' assets are from entities that are governed by ERISA and the Plan Asset Regulations ("benefit plan investors"), then the fund will not be able to claim a certain exception under ERISA which allows it to avoid all of the fund's assets being deemed "Plan Assets" in terms of ERISA and the regulations.

BENEFIT PLAN INVESTORS:

For the purposes of counting your 25 percent, a Benefit Plan Investor is not only an investor who is governed by ERISA. It includes any employee benefit plan,

individual retirement plans, Keogh plans, and any entity that itself has more than 25 percent investment by Benefit Plans such as, for example, another hedge fund!

The maze of definitions, exceptions and un-exceptions is not practically important; what is important is that there are serious consequences to the fund if the number of ERISA investors exceeds the 25 percent mark.

If that were to happen, the following minimum level of restrictions would apply:

- The investment manager would now be classified as a fiduciary and would have to comply with the extensive requirements and restrictions applicable to fiduciaries under ERISA. (It's well beyond the scope of this guide to go into detail here, but essentially we are talking about the kind of restrictions you would expect to be applied to someone looking after a retirement plan: at every point of the process, you

should be asking whether this is the right investment for this particular plan, is it sufficiently safe, diversified, appropriate, liquid, etc.)

- The fund's activities would be subject to the prohibited transactions of ERISA, which include a prohibition against transactions with affiliates; and performance fees would probably need to be adjusted.

- In all likelihood, the benefit plan investors would divest their holdings in the fund, as they tend to invest in hedge funds in order to place part of their portfolio outside of the restrictive rules governing Plan Assets.

There are a few peculiarities that need to be taken into account when doing the calculation.

HOW TO COUNT TO 25%

- The limit applies to each class within the fund, not just to the fund as a whole. It is possible, therefore, for the total percentage to be well below 25 percent

but for a given class to tip the scales, thereby contaminating the entire fund.

- A Benefit Plan Investor includes entities which aren't governed by ERISA (see box above); make sure you're counting them, too.

- Assets held by the investment manager, the founder of the investment manager, and any affiliate of those entities and people, are to be excluded from the calculation. Given that co-investment by the IM is an important element of most funds, this can constitute a significant chunk of the fund's assets over time and can drastically alter the percentage of Plan Assets within the fund.

CHAPTER 17

CONCLUSION

There are a few ways to protect against this risk and a few things to watch out for. The first, of course, is not to accept Plan Assets as investors in the first place. This has its place, but is inappropriate for most funds. The second way is to cap ERISA investors at a very low threshold so that you vastly reduce the risk of hitting the 25 percent ceiling (I have seen this as low as 10 percent).

What you should not do, however, is pretend that you are not at risk, and neglect to keep track of the level of Plan Assets in your fund. I have seen funds realize, just as they were processing a redemption, that if they continued to process the redemption, their Plan Assets would be just over the threshold, and they had to suspend the redemption until the following Dealing Day when they knew they had additional subscriptions coming in to ensure the Plan Assets stayed below the level. From that point on, calculating the level was performed every month by both the investment manager and the administrator and any differences were debated with as much vigor as a difference in the NAV!

Every fund that accepts benefit plan investors needs to have a rigorous process in place to monitor and track the level of Plan Assets within the fund. Speak to your onshore law firm about the consequences and risks, and speak to your administrator to identify best practices and tools for monitoring your levels.

CHAPTER EIGHTTEEN

CHAPTER 18
Next Steps, Front Shore and the Companion Website and Newsletter

So now that you've finished the book you're ready to set your fund up! If you have any questions at all, I'm available to answer them at Gordon.casey@frontshore.com, and so is the team at Front Shore, who you can find at www.frontshore.com

But if you want to explore this some more and stay informed of changes, get some additional resources, then go to www.gordoncasey.com, download the tools that are available on the site and please sign up for the newsletter.

The companion website will mainly serve to house a live, updated version of the information included in the book, especially the stuff in the Appendices.

The information that will be published in the newsletter and housed on the website expands on and compliments the information in this guide, and most of it is freely downloadable (some will only be sent via the newsletter). Many of the documents are provided in a format that will enable you to use them as templates for your own fund.

WWW.GORDONCASEY.COM

AP
PEN
DIX

APPENDIX
Costs

Here is a list of cost ranges that you can expect to pay for a variety of elements involved in the establishment of your Cayman fund.

Note that the government fees and fees payable to CIMA are fixed as of the date of publication, but they are subject to change (and they change frequently, and by "change" I mean "increase").

We are also only giving the fees for companies with an authorized share capital of less than $50,000. Larger authorized share capitals lead to greater fees. The service provider fees are, of course, indicative. Please visit our Resources page at www.gordoncasey.com for the latest information we have available in this regard.

FEES PAYABLE TO THE GENERAL REGISTRY [1]

Upon Establishment

- Exempted Limited Liability Company $731.71

- Exempt Limited Partnership $1,219.51

- Trust $609.76

- Exempted Segregated Portfolio Company $1,341.46

Annually by the end of March

- Exempted Limited Liability Company $853.66

- Exempt Limited Partnership $1,463.41

- Trust $609.76

- Exempted Segregated Portfolio Company $3,292.68

One-off fees for documentation and penalties

In the event that you require additional documentation, or need to file new documents at the Registry, you will need to pay fees for each filing or document. This is a rather long list and we've decided not to print it here, but we encourage you to check online or with your registered agent for these costs.

Late filing of documentation or payment of annual fees will lead to penalties charged to the fund.

APPENDIX

---

1 You can also visit
www.ciregistry.gov.ky/pls/portal/docs/PAGE/REGHOME/FEES/GENERAL%20REGISTRY%20FEES%20SCHEDULE.PDF for this information

FEES PAYABLE TO CIMA [2]

Initial registration fees

Exempted Fund and
Closed-End Fund
nothing

Registered Fund
*$365.85 filing fee + $4,268.29
for first year of registration,
or part thereof.*

Licensed Fund
*$365.85 filing fee + $4,268.29
for first year of registration,
or part thereof.*

Administered Fund
*$365.85 filing fee + $4,268.29
for first year of registration,
or part thereof.*

Master Fund
*$365.85 filing fee + $3,048.78
for first year of registration,
or part thereof.*

Segregated Portfolio Company
per portfolio, up to a
maximum of 25 portfolios
*an additional fee of $304.88
for first year of registration,
or part thereof.*

Excluded Manager
*$6,097.56 for first year
of registration, or part thereof.*

Licensed Manager
*$609.76 filing fee + $9,756.10
on granting of license.*

Annual fees

Exempted and
Closed-Ended Funds
not applicable.

Registered Fund
*$365.85 Funds Annual Return
filing fee + $4,268.29 per year.*

Licensed Fund
*$365.85 Funds Annual Return
filing fee + $4,268.29 per year.*

Administered Fund
*$365.85 Funds Annual Return
filing fee + $4,268.29 per year.*

Master Fund
*$365.85 Funds Annual Return
filing fee + $3,048.78 per year.*

Segregated Portfolio Company
per portfolio, up to a maximum of 25 portfolios
*$365.85 Funds Annual Return
filing fee + $304.88 per year.*

Exempted Manager
$6,097.56 per year

Licensed Manager
$9,756.10 per year.

---

2 These fees are also published online at
www.cimoney.com.ky/regulated_sectors/reg_sec_ra.aspx?id=246

FEES PAYABLE TO THE REGISTERED OFFICE [3]

Incorporation Fees
between $500 and $2,000

Annual Fees
between $250 and $2,000

Set fees
registered offices also have set fees for specific post-incorporation activities, such as filing fees, requests for specific documents and so on.

Hourly rates
between $50 and $200 per hour

FEES PAYABLE TO OFFSHORE LAW FIRMS

Fund Set up [4]
between $8,000 and $25,000 depending on the scope of the services to be provided and the complexity of the fund structure, strategy, and offering.

Hourly rates
between $200 and $950 per hour.

FEES PAYABLE TO ADMINISTRATORS

Minimum

Most administrators have a monthly minimum that would apply while the fund is still raising capital. I have seen this as low as $2,500 per month and as high as $10,000.

Basis points

The normal fees charged by the admins are in basis points, as in thousandths of a percentage point. Depending on the complexity of the fund and the scope of services that are being provided by the administrator, fees are generally charged on a declining scale, with the highest fee applicable to the first tranche of capital in the fund. For example, you might see 15 bps for the first $25 million, 12 bps for assets between $25 and $50 million, and so on, down to perhaps 8 bps for assets over $250 million.

---

3 Note that not all fees are created equal — some of the incorporation fees include a larger initial document pack, and some are inclusive of all time spent. The same goes for the annual fees; the fee arrangement should be examined closely and fully understood before entering into a relationship with your registered office or you could be in for a big surprise at the end of the incorporation process or your first year.

4 Usually including drafting, review and filing of all offering documentation.

AUDIT FEES

Fixed fee

The standard procedure has historically been for the audit to be a fixed fee determined by the complexity of the strategy, the number of trades, the difficulty of valuation and so on. Traditionally, we would see audits range between the firms from as low as $16,000 up to $40,000 or so.

Progressive fee

Recently, the majority of audit firms have agreed to progressive rates for emerging managers, with a low fee that progresses up to their 'standard rate' either on the basis of time alone, or on the basis of the assets under management. In this context I have seen fees start as low as $8,000 for the first year, or first $10 million.

FRONT SHORE FEES?

Set up fees

As far as we know, we're the only firm that is exclusively focused on project management of offshore fund setups (please let us know if you hear of anybody else doing the same thing, we'd love to meet them!) We charge a fixed fee for fund and manager setups, based on the number of entities, parties and jurisdictions involved. Fees range from $7,500 up to $35,000.

Ongoing monthly retainer

A number of our clients ask us to stick around for a while after the setup is complete, sometimes for a few months just to check that everything worked out the way we all thought, and sometimes for years, to be available for pretty much anything else that comes up and could do with an external resource that is ready to jump at a moment's notice. Our fees vary largely for this service but they start at about $500 a month.

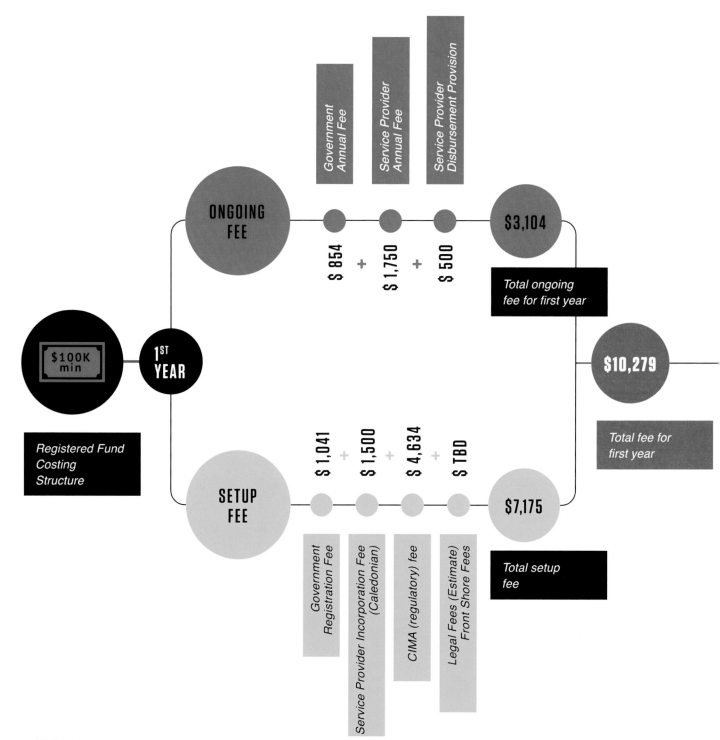

Registered Fund Costing Structure

$100K min

1ST YEAR

ONGOING FEE

Government Annual Fee
Service Provider Annual Fee
Service Provider Disbursement Provision

$ 854 + $ 1,750 + $ 500

$3,104

Total ongoing fee for first year

SETUP FEE

$ 1,041 + $ 1,500 + $ 4,634 + $ TBD

Government Registration Fee
Service Provider Incorporation Fee (Caledonian)
CIMA (regulatory) fee
Legal Fees (Estimate) Front Shore Fees

$7,175

Total setup fee

$10,279

Total fee for first year

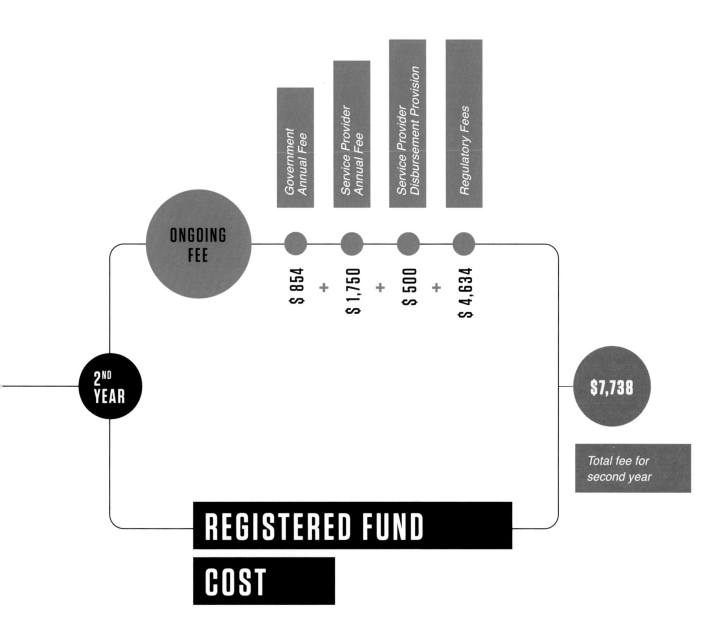

ONGOING FEE

Government Annual Fee

Service Provider Annual Fee

Service Provider Disbursement Provision

Regulatory Fees

$ 854 + $ 1,750 + $ 500 + $ 4,634

2ND YEAR

$7,738

Total fee for second year

REGISTERED FUND

COST

AP
PEN
DIX II

APPENDIX II
Resources

There are a huge number of resources available online, starting with the companion website to this book at www.gordoncasey.com, which includes updated information

on all of the costs and other details included in these appendices, including the official, governmental and CIMA websites which also contain a great deal of information. On top of that, industry organizations, such as AIMA and the MFA, contain guidelines that may be useful to you but are beyond the scope of this guide.

On our website at www. gordoncasey.com we've included links to one or two articles and other resources on topics covered in Section II of this guide. Good articles on these topics are surprisingly hard to come by and even harder to find via traditional search methods online, so we thought we'd give you a bit of a head start.

HA 100% ALL-TIME-GUARANTEED COMPREHENSIVE LIST. NOT.

Legislation[1]

on the CIMA website contains, as far as I can tell, all of the relevant legislation that you will ever need. There is guidance as well, so explore the rest of the site.

Forms

We're still on the CIMA website. You'll need to know which form you need for your fund in order to download the right one (see Chapter One), but here are all the forms you need to complete: **www.cimoney.com.ky/regulated_sectors/reg_sec_ra.aspx?id=248**

GENERAL INFORMATION ON CAYMAN

Registry

www.ciregistry.gov.ky/portal/page?_pageid=3521,1&_dad=portal&_schema=PORTAL and more on Companies, Partnerships and Trusts is available through the links on the website.

CIMA WEBSITE:

www.cimoney.com.ky/ is a great source of information and guidelines, but you'll have to do a bit of exploring to extract all of the value possible. The main fund section is at **www.cimoney.com.ky/regulated_sectors/reg_sec.aspx?id=96** and we have links to other important sections elsewhere. Don't neglect to download the AML Guidance [2] and the recently published Statement of Guidance on Corporate Governance for Mutual Funds [3]

---

1 www.cimoney.com.ky/regulatory_framework/reg_frame_law_reg.aspx?id=372
2 www.cimoney.com.ky/AML_CFT/aml_cft.aspx?id=144
3 You have to search for SOG next to the title on this page
   www.cimoney.com.ky/regulatory_framework/reg_frame_ra.aspx?id=1746&ekmensel=e2f22c9a_16_92_1746_5
   Notes: http://www.cimoney.com.ky/AML_CFT/aml_cft.aspx?id=144. CIMA also has an FAQ at http://www.cimoney.com.ky/regulated_sectors/reg_sec_ra.aspx?id=244.

FEES

The fees payable to the Registry are contained on their website at **www.ciregistry.gov.ky/portal/** **page?_pageid=3521,6697168&_dad=portal&_schema=PORTAL** and the CIMA fees applicable to your fund or manager are available at **www.cimoney.com.ky/regulated_sectors/reg_sec_ra.aspx?id=246.**

AIMA INDUSTRY GUIDES:

The Alternative Investment Management Association has been one of the leading self-regulatory bodies in the hedge fund industry since its inception in 1990. Along with other great work that it does, it produces guidelines that are extremely helpful in maintaining best practices at your fund. A lot of them are available free to the public, and some require you to be a member to access them, or to pay. You should consider membership, of course, but feel free to browse through their list of publications on their website at **aima.org/en/education/aima-guides.cfm.**

MFA GUIDELINES:

The Managed Funds Association is another great organization within the industry. Traditionally more U.S.-focused than AIMA, their website also has a lot of fantastic resources for new managers. A good starting point is their homepage[4] and their Global Fund Regulation page[5] has some good links at the bottom of the page if you want to explore certain issues further.

CAYMAN STOCK EXCHANGE:

The website for the CSX[6] has all of the listing rules and guidelines available. Unfortunately I can't link to individual pages, but the information is quite clearly marked in the left-hand menu.

---

4 www.managedfunds.org
5 www.managedfunds.org/issues-policy/issues/globalhedge-fund-regulation
6 www.csx.com.ky

FATCA

KPMG

KPMG has a lot of really great, comprehensive, resources for fund managers. I like this brochure on FATCA and the fund industry: www.kpmg.com/ Global/en/IssuesAndInsights/ ArticlesPublications/Pages/ fatca- and-the-funds-industry. aspx

EY's

EY's FATCA section is great too, check it out here: **www. ey.com/GL/en/Industries/ Financial-Services/Banking- --Capital-Markets/FATCA- -resources** and here: **www. ey.com/GL/en/Industries/ Financial-Services/Banking--- Capital-Markets/FATCA--tools**

OTHER LINKS

I'm roaming beyond the specifics of the Cayman Islands now, but there are just a few other links that you should be aware are out there. In case you haven't come across them already, I hope these help.

The Village Albourne[7] is a news collector and community that has been around for a very long time (far longer than the more snazzy, professional news sites I refer to below). It's a free, and fantastic, resource and I highly recommend it. Check out their library for a wealth of information, and explore the site as much as you can — it's got a great 90s feel, too!

HFMWeek is a weekly news publication covering everything in the industry; check out the online version at **www.hfm-week.com.**

The Hedge Fund Association is a U.S.-based, international lobbying organization. You can read more at **thehfa.org.**

---

7 village.albourne.com/village/login

HedgeWorld [8] is a news and research portal. It's also got a community section and a daily newsletter. They also run a couple of conferences every year.

HedgeAnswers [9] is a place where you can pose questions and get answers; beyond that they have quite a few initiatives that should be helpful to start-up managers.

Operations for Alternatives is a recently launched site and community resource that aims to provide a single, definitive source of information for people in the alternative funds industry. I've just joined this one and hope to contribute to, and gain from, the process. Check it out at **www.ofa-america.com**.

HedgeCo.net is a database of fund information and also includes some great tools for new managers. **www.hedgeco.net** for the main site and **www.hedgeco. net/hedgeducation/hedge-fund-articles** for their articles on the industry in general. Their conference page is a great place to see how many fund conferences are going on at any given time! [10]

---

8 www.hedgeworld.com
9 www.hedgeanswers.com
10 www.hedgeco.net/conferences/hedge-fund-conferences.php

APPENDIX III

APPENDIX III
Contact Details

Front Shore can be a great help with the crucial task of identifying the right service provider for your particular needs, and obtaining quotes from various parties; but if you're ready to go it alone, you're going to need to get in touch with some service providers.

The following list is as comprehensive a list of service providers that we could come up with. Naturally, there are operators in each of these categories spread around the world and I wasn't able to identify everyone who is participating in the marketplace (they are welcome to contact me for inclusion in the next edition of the book, or on the website).

For all but a very few of the companies listed below, I can provide a personal introduction to a director or partner at each of these firms, otherwise, their contact details are available via their websites.

So, once you've looked through their website, if you like, just email me at **Gordon.casey@frontshore.com** and ask for an introduction and I'll put you in touch with the right person right away. Some of these details might change in time, you can view or download an up to date version of this list on **www.gordoncasey.com**.

ADMINISTRATORS

Admiral
admiraladmin.com

Amicorp
amicorp-funds.com

Apex
apexfundservices.com

Atlas
atlasfundservices.com

Augentius
augentius.com

Circle Partners
circlepartners.com

Citco
citco.com/divisions/fund-services

Citi
citibank.com/transactionservices/
home/securities_svcs/fund/fa.jsp

Credit Suisse
credit-suisse.com/investment_
banking/client_offering/en/
hedge_funds.jsp

Intertrust
intertrustgroup.com/en/funds

Mitsubishi
(formerly Butterfield Fulcrum)
mitsubishiufjfundservices.com

Northern Trust
northerntrust.com/asset-
servicing/united-states/services/
fund-services

SGGG
sgggfsi.com or sgggfsicayman.ky

SS&C
sscglobeop.com

Trident
tridentfundservices.com

UBS
ubs.com/global/en/asset_
management/fundservices.html

AUDITORS

Baker Tilly
bakertillycayman.com

BDO
bdo.ky

Deloitte & Touche
deloitte.com/ky

EY
ey.com/KY/en

Grant Thornton
gtcayman.com

Kinetic Partners
kinetic-partners.com/
jurisdictions/cayman-islands-
services/

KPMG
kpmg.com/ky/en/pages/
default.aspx

KPMG Curacao
kpmg.com/dutchcaribbean/en/
pages/default.aspx[1]

PKF
pkfcayman.com

PricewaterhouseCoopers
pwc.com/ky/en

Weiser Mazars
weisermazars.com (and look up
the Cayman office)

BANKS

Butterfield
ky.butterfieldgroup.com

Caledonian
caledonian.com/banking

DMS Bank
dmsoffshore.com/services/
banking-custody/

FCIB/CIBC
cibcfcib.com

HSBC
hsbc.ky

RBC
rbcroyalbank.com/caribbean/
cayman/home.html

INDEPENDENT DIRECTORS

Appleby Trust
applebyglobal.com

ARC Directors
arcdirectors.com

Bell Rock
bellrockcs.com

DMS
dmsoffshore.com

Eclipse
eclipseconsultingllc.com

Front Shore
frontshore.com (but you
knew that already right?)

Highwater
highwater.ky

**International Management
Services (IMS)**
ims.ky

Intertrust Cayman
intertrustgroup.com/en/
locations/cayman-islands

Management Plus
mplgroup.com

Maples Fiduciary Services
maplesfs.com

MG Management
mgcayman.com

Ogier Fiduciary Services
ogier.com/Services/
Administration/Corporate-
Services/Pages/Default.aspx

OFFSHORE LAW FIRMS IN CAYMAN [2]

Campbells
www.campbells.com.ky

Conyers Dill & Pearman
conyersdill.com

Dillon Eustace
dilloneustace.ie

Harneys
harneys.com

Maples
maplesandcalder.com

Mourant Ozannes
mourantozannes.com

---

1 I've included the Curacao team specifically due to their longevity and expertise in the industry, please contact me for a personal introduction.
2 Please contact me so I can provide personal introductions to the appropriate partner at any these firms
3 There are lots more, these are the ones that focus on funds and with which I have personal experience

Ogier
ogier.com

Priestleys
palawcayman.com

Smeets Law
smeetslawnet.com

Solomon Harris
solomonharris.com

Walkers
walkersglobal.com

OPERATIONAL DUE DILIGENCE CONSULTANTS

Albourne Partners
albourne.com

Beaumont Advisors
beaumontadvisors.com

Castle Hall Alternatives
castlehallalternatives.com

REGISTERED OFFICE AND REGISTERED AGENTS [3]

Caledonian
caledonian.com

Citco
citco.com

DMS
dmsoffshore.com

Maples Fiduciary
maplesfs.com

Ogier Fiduciary
ogier.com/Services/
Administration/Corporate-
Services/Pages/Default.aspx

Portcullis TrustNet
portcullis-trustnet.com

Trident
ridenttrust.com

AP PEN DIX IV

APPENDIX IV
Template Documents

You can find workable versions of the following documents online at the companion website at www.gordoncasey.com.

In addition to the basic documents included here, the website has sample completed forms for you to peruse as you're completing your own forms, and draft Mems and Arts, along with specific wording for certain sections of the PPM.

Launch resolution, resolution appointing first shareholders and directors, completed MF1, letter of resignation, letter/resolution accepting appointment, auditors and administrators consent letter, certificate.

APPENDIX V

APPENDIX V
AML and KYC

The anti-money laundering (AML) and know-your-customer (KYC) requirements that apply to most service providers operating in the offshore fund industry are quite stringent.

If your only experience of a personal due diligence exercise has been with your local, neighborhood bank, prepare to feel a little violated or offended by the amount of documentation you may have to produce to prove that you are who you say you are, and you're not a crook, and your company is owned by who you say owns it, and so on.

The obligation to ensure that clients are not laundering money has grown exponentially over the past 15 years. The primary method that your service providers will use to achieve this assurance is through documentation.

At the outset, you're going to have a range of people and companies looking for various documents in slightly different numbers and formats. This can be both frustrating and confusing, especially when you send it off and then get asked for what seems to be the same thing again.

Front Shore has a great service (part and parcel of fund establishment service) where we compile all of the document requests into one large request, draft and prepare the letters of reference and then discuss the process with you to determine who will be doing what, and then send you detailed, specific and personal instructions on everything you need to provide. We then distribute that to all of the parties, and you're done!

Unless you've been through this process already, you won't be able to appreciate the amount of time and frustration this saves.

If you've ever been involved in establishing relationships and have had difficulties with the KYC process, and the people you have dealt with appeared stubborn, we feel your pain. But they really are just doing their jobs and their jobs are pretty much dictated by global legal and regulatory standards.

In essence, they are looking to do a few things: to have an individual person associated with every account (the so-called ultimate beneficial owner, or UBO) and to have proof that the individual person is an actual person, and is the actual person that they are dealing with.

Once they have that, they can comply with their other obligations by putting that name in their system and running all of the names in their system through various databases to check if there is any illegal activity associated with any of those names.

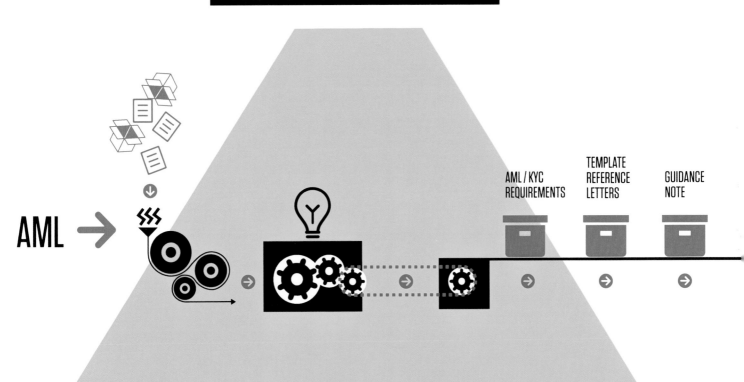

AML & KYC (IF I'M HELPING YOU)

AML

AML / KYC REQUIREMENTS

TEMPLATE REFERENCE LETTERS

GUIDANCE NOTE

APPENDIX VI

Yes, it's true, there are other places where you can set up your fund. There are loads actually.

Cayman has soared in popularity over the past decade or so, but there are many others that are still extremely active, have great legislation and regulation and, very importantly, quality service providers. I wanted to highlight just a few, select jurisdictions here. The idea is to give you a little background on the regulatory structure of each jurisdiction and an indication of any additional information that may be good to know, mostly as a demonstration of the variety of options that are out there.

BVI

BVI is a small place with a progressive approach to fund regulation and legislation. They have a similar regulatory model to Cayman, with the possibility to offer funds to a limited number of investors (Private Funds — below 50 investors), focused on professional, high-net worth investors (Professional Funds) and public funds. All three types of fund are required to submit their documentation, and pay a fee, to the regulatory body in the BVI, the Financial Services Commission. (Only closed-ended funds are exempt from regulation.)

BVI funds are all required to appoint an investment manager, an administrator, a custodian and an auditor. They are also required to have at least two directors, one of whom must be an individual.

They also have recently introduced a new regulatory regime for fund managers, called the Approved Manager Regime. Subject to certain restrictions, submission of the application form, together with payment entitles the investment manager to provide management services to BVI-recognized funds without waiting for approval from the Financial Services Commission. And I believe that is set to extend to non-BVI funds with equivalent regulations, as recognized by the FSC (and including Cayman) in 2014.

IRELAND

Ireland has seen tremendous growth in its fund industry in the past 15 years, due to sound regulation and a level of service provider excellence that is extremely impressive (I might be biased here, my name is Casey...).

In addition to UCITS funds, which are available throughout Europe, the Irish regulator authorizes Professional Investor Funds (PIF), with a minimum investment of EUR 125,000 and a limited number of investment restrictions; and Qualifying Investor Funds (QIF) with virtually no investment restrictions and a minimum investment of EUR 250,000.

All Irish funds are required to have quite a number of Irish-resident service providers, including two directors, the administrator, a custodian, legal advisor and auditor. Similar to a lot of other jurisdictions, the fund will have to file a prospectus and it will take up to 6 weeks to get approval from the regulator.

MALTA

In addition to the usual European structures available, Malta offers three types of Professional Investment Funds (PIF), with varying levels of regulatory scrutiny and restrictions.

Funds may be marketed to Experienced Investors (the lowest threshold of professional investor, subject to a minimum investment of EUR 10,000), Qualifying Investors (the middle level, requiring the investor to have net assets greater than EUR 750,000 and a minimum investment of EUR 75,000), and Extraordinary Investors (the highest level, restricted to those investors with a net worth greater than EUR 7.5 million and subject to a minimum investment of EUR 750,000).

PIF's marketed to Experienced Investors may not leverage their position by more than 100 percent and have certain other restrictions as well. PIF's marketed to Qualifying Investors have no investment restrictions but must issue a comprehensive Offering Document (PPM), unlike those marketed to Extraordinary Investors, which only require a simplified marketing document.

Jersey has a long list of fund types and spans the full range in terms of regulatory touch. But the approach, while more intricate than other jurisdictions, should be familiar to you by now. Jersey makes a distinction between Certified Funds, which must comply with Codes of Conduct, and uncertified funds, which have no such obligation. Looking at the list below, Expert, Listed and Unclassified Funds are all Certified Funds.

Recognized Funds are highly regulated and may be marketed to the public; the usual restrictions and comprehensive guidelines apply to these funds.

Unclassified Funds are those that are restricted to 50 investors or those that are offered to the public and do not meet other definitions. They also have fairly comprehensive regulation and oversight.

Listed Funds are exactly what they sound like; they require two resident directors and a resident manager or administrator, amongst other stringent requirements.

Expert Funds are marketed to investors that are self-acknowledged "experts" and are subject to a $100,000 minimum investment. There are residency requirements for these funds, too (in terms of local directors, managers and/or administrators).

Private Placement Funds are closed-ended funds for professional-type investors that can avail of a fast-track authorization process, provided they meet certain requirements laid out by the Jersey regulator.

Very Private Funds – I love the name of this fund structure. These are investment vehicles for 15 investors or fewer and they are virtually un-regulated. The idea here is that these essentially amount to joint ventures between the investors.

Unregulated Funds – These funds must file a notice with the regulator with some essential details but are otherwise, unsurprisingly, unregulated. They include two types of fund: Unregulated Eligible Investor Funds (for professional-type investors) and Unregulated Exchange-Traded Funds (which must be closed-ended and listed).

CURAÇAO

Curacao is one of the oldest offshore fund jurisdictions and was quite innovative during its heyday. It is reclaiming some of that reputation slowly as it seeks to cater to new and emerging markets such as Latin America, Africa, and Sharia investors.

Unlike most of the other jurisdictions, Curacao does not have a finite list of fund types but rather requires that both the documentation and personnel for each fund is submitted to the regulator (the Central Bank) for approval prior to launch. While this makes things a little opaque from a planning point of view, it encourages innovation from the local service providers and dialogue with the regulator from day one.

The strength of Curacao as a jurisdiction is right there with the service providers who have a remarkable wealth of experience in the industry, and the strong checks and balances inherent within the approval process.

APPENDIX VII

A Brief History of Offshore Hedge Funds

The history of hedge funds itself is a fascinating story and almost immediately begs the question of what puts the 'hedge' in hedge fund. So, avoiding that mini-controversy, let's focus on the offshore funds industry as a whole, without paying too much attention to whether or not the strategies involved can really justify including the funds under the "hedge fund" moniker.

ALFRED W. JONES

If you want to know where it all began then you have to start, wrongly or rightly, with Alfred W. Jones. While Jones may not have come up with the concept of the first hedge fund (there were academic papers similar to his strategy as early as the 1920s), he is certainly the most well-known early adopter of the most well-known hedge fund strategy: a balanced portfolio of stocks that is long on stocks that are expected to go up in value, and short on stocks that are expected to go down in value.

Apparently Jones himself (a sociologist and a financial journalist) referred to his strategy as being "hedged" against exposure to overall market movement.

By the 50s, Jones was charging the fund (a limited partnership) a 20 percent performance fee — the second key feature that, in most cases, distinguishes a hedge fund from another form of investment vehicle.

Jones became famous, and spawned a number of copycat funds, when an article was written on him and his fund in Fortune magazine in 1966, and, within a few years, there were hundreds of funds, and funds-of-funds spread throughout the world.

GOING OFFSHORE

One of the first funds to go offshore was the Quantum group of funds, started in Curacao in the early 70s by George Soros and Jim Rogers (who writes some great books while he tours the world on his motorbike).

One of the primary reasons why funds went offshore was, unsurprisingly, to reduce the tax and regulatory burden on the fund and its investors, particularly where the manager was based in the U.S. but the fund's investors were not (or not all of them were).

Prior to 1997, U.S. tax laws stipulated that there were ten administrative activities that needed to be performed outside of the U.S. if the fund wanted to avoid attracting U.S. federal tax.

What were the 10 Commandments?

1. Communicating with shareholders.

2. Communicating with the public.

3. Soliciting sales of shares.

4. Accepting subscriptions from new investors.

5. Maintaining corporate records and books of account.

6. Auditing of the books of account.

7. Disbursement of dividends, legal fees, accounting fees and directors' salaries.

8. Publishing and furnishing the offering and redemption prices of its shares.

9. Conducting meetings of shareholders and directors.

10. Making redemptions of its shares.

You may have noticed, in scanning through that list, that the vast majority of those activities are performed by the fund administrator — and indeed, the need for these activities to be maintained offshore is what gave birth to the hedge fund administration business.

At a later stage, certainly by 1997, fund administrators were also crucial in providing an independent verification of the fund's NAV, and the repeal of the 10 commandments did not, as some feared, kill the fund administration business at all. On the contrary, the net result was that administrators moved onshore, closer to their clients and provided an increasing array of services to funds and fund managers; eventually offering a full "front to back" suite for those who wanted it.

Post 2008 financial crisis (meltdown?), some of the creative accounting practices that certain managers had engaged in were revealed and it is now the norm for all funds, onshore and offshore, to engage independent fund administrators.

Long Term Capital Management

This is the granddaddy of hedge fund blow-ups and a story that anyone in the industry should be familiar with (I highly recommend the great book When Genius Failed for anybody interested in knowing all the details).

But the truth is that there is no real scandal here — to put it simply, a private investment company (a fund) didn't understand its risk profile properly, was overexposed, and lost a huge amount of money.

The scandal, per se, was the effect that all of this had on the other players in the business. In a move that turned out to just be the prequel to "Too Big to Fail," Wall Street cobbled a bail-out of sorts for the fund in order to prevent systemic failures taking hold.

To offer a little more detail, LTCM was the manager of a fund founded in 1994 by an ex-Salomon Brother's trader and run by him, two Nobel laureates and other extremely important and influential members of the investment industry.

By 1998, the fund had been extremely successful with its strategy, a bond arbitrage strategy that took advantage of minute differences in bond pricing, but was seeking more aggressive trades globally in order to continue delivering results on the almost $5 billion that investors had placed with them.

Placing hugely leveraged positions exaggerated the relatively small risks they were taking exponentially: if you take into account the underlying value of the assets on which the derivatives they traded were based, the notional value of their positions was over $1 trillion.

As a confluence of crises forced the value of their investments to decline, LTCM were faced with a liquidity crisis: they had to unload investments at precisely the wrong moment. Immediately before they were bailed out, their assets had shrunk to $400 million.

On 23 September 1998 the New York Federal Reserve coordinated a bailout that essentially allowed for a coordinated liquidation of the company, avoiding the systematic failure that everyone feared. Although there has been criticism for the out-sized risk that was allowed to creep into the market through LTCM's strategy, clearly all parties share some responsibility for that and, based on the current global financial crisis, it could be said that no real lessons were learned.

The Manhattan Investment Fund

A pre-cursor to the Madoff scandal, the Manhattan fund fabricated investment results when huge losses were suffered in the late 90s. Although the bet was correct (a short position on IT stocks), the bubble outlasted the strategy and rather than report the losses that were being suffered, the fund's manager, Michael Berger, hid the $400 million of losses from the fund's investors.

Berger was charged and found guilty in 2000 but skipped bail, only to turn up in Austria in 2005, where he managed to avoid being extradited back to the U.S.

Madoff

So what did Bernie Madoff do? Let's ignore the question of whether he started out trying to defraud investors back in 1960 when he founded his company, or when exactly his strategy changed to "cheating," and instead answer the small question of what fraud he actually committed. In essence, he fabricated investment results. He made them up and told investors that the fund was getting better returns than it actually was.

Once that was the case, it was the usual Ponzi situation where new funds sustain the illusion of profitability and success (new investors' money would be used to pay out investors that were redeeming out of the fund).

What's the lesson we should learn from all of this? Almost all of the people involved in the Madoff fund were family or very close to family; and the auditor was mostly non-existent and certainly not an established auditor. It's highly likely that just the most basic corporate governance standards would have unearthed the fraud or prevented it from happening in the first place: independent oversight by a board of directors, an independent administrator and a proper audit.

Weavering

The Weavering case was, sadly, just another fraud — fake deals to generated fake returns, generating greater fees for the manager and gathering more investor assets. The interesting thing about the Weavering case is that the directors of the offshore fund entity, based in Cayman, were fined $111 million each (!) in relation to the losses suffered by the fund's investors.

The two directors were related to the fund's UK-based manager (who was also found personally liable by a UK court) and the message here is clear as well: independent directors that are capable of ensuring that the fund engages in effective corporate governance are a key requirement for all funds.

The Offshore Jurisdictions

Prior to 2000, the leading offshore jurisdiction for hedge funds was almost certainly Curacao, home to Quantum, Permal and a number of other large funds, and also to Citco, the world's largest fund administrator.

BVI was already, at that point, overtaking Curacao and had adopted flexible legislation and regulation that allowed it to get funds up and running far quicker, and more transparently, than Curacao, and Cayman was adopting the BVI model as well.

Over the course of the 2000s a number of jurisdictions globally competed for fund business; Ireland and Luxembourg emerged as the clear market leaders within the European market, but Cayman has come out on top as the global leader by an order of magnitude, home to, by some estimates, as much as 34 percent of all of the funds established worldwide (onshore and offshore).

It's hard to pinpoint the exact cause of Cayman's success but it's a combination, I believe, of regulatory and legislative creativity and flexibility, consolidation and excellence within the service provider market generally and, after a certain point, reaching a tipping point where it just became the de facto leader, and you now have to justify yourself if you are NOT establishing your fund in Cayman.

APPENDIX VIII

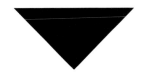

APPENDIX VIII
Glossary of Terms and Abbreviations

AIFMD (The Alternative Investment Fund Managers Directive)

(an EU directive) See Chapter Sixteen for all the juicy details.

AIMA (Alternative Investment Management Association)

An industry body dedicated to development, leadership and guidance within the alternative fund industry. See their website at **www.aima.org.**

AML (Anti-Money Laundering)

Global initiatives, legislation, regulation, and internal policy all touch on AML – the goal being to reduce and ultimately eliminate the ability of criminals and criminal networks to move funds that are the proceeds of crime through the banking system and, thereby, give them a seemingly legitimate provenance. This process is known as money laundering, and any activities that have the goal of preventing that are part and parcel of AML.

CIMA (Cayman Islands Monetary Authority)

The main regulatory body in the Cayman Islands, CIMA is responsible for overseeing the fund industry there, including funds, managers, and administrators.

Dealing Day

In most cases a Dealing Day is the day on which shares in the fund may be subscribed for, or redeemed. In some cases, a fund may accept subscriptions and process redemptions at different frequencies, in which case they will be referred to as Subscription Days and Redemption Days (or something similar).

ERISA (Employee Retirement Income Security Act)

A piece of legislation that, among other things, governs how retirement funds may be invested. See Chapter Seventeen – ERISA for more details.

FATCA (the Foreign Account Tax Compliance Act)

U.S. legislation with global implications. Read all about it in Chapter Fifteen.

FFI (Foreign Financial Institution)

A term defined under FATCA. These are the entities that will need to register with the IRS and file information or face withholding on U.S. Source income.

Gate

This is the ability to Lock-up shares, and investors, under certain circumstances, such as market emergencies, a higher level of redemptions than the fund can pay out due to liquidity issues and so on.

GIIN (Global Intermediary Identification Number)

The number that an FFI will be issued with when it registers with the IRS under FATCA using their wonderful online portal.

IGA (Inter-Governmental Agreement)

An agreement between the IRS and another country concerning the implementation of FATCA within that country. There are various models of IGA out there and the IGA with Cayman is a so-called Model 1 agreement, similar to the IGA with the UK.

IM (Investment Manager)

Also known as the investment advisor or simply the manager, or advisor. IMA: Investment Management Agreement. See Chapter Five.

KYC (Know Your Customer)

This phrase refers to the various processes and procedures that companies must go through in order to satisfy the due diligence requirements of the regulatory body which they are governed by, as well as their own internal policies. As the basic requirement is to identify, and obtain proof of, the ultimate client, it is called KYC.

Lock-up

If you are not able to redeem your shares for a specific amount of time after subscription, then the fund has a lock-up period. Some funds may have soft lock-ups, where redemptions are permitted but come with a penalty fee (for example, it may have a three-year lock-up with penalty fees of 3 percent in the first year, 2 percent in the second year, and 1 percent in the third year). It is also possible for redemptions to be suspended in extreme circumstances (stock market crash, global liquidity crisis) and at such a time the fund may be referred to as being in a lock-up.

MFA (Managed Funds Association)

An industry body and lobbying organization. See Appendix II – Resourcess for more details.

Management Fee

A fee levied by the investment manager against the assets under management by the fund. Management fees will generally be between 1 percent and 2 percent per year of the total assets in the fund, payable monthly.

Management Shares

Shares issued to a separate company for the purpose of controlling administrative issues that, in terms of the fund's Memorandum and Articles, require shareholder approval. They are non-participating, meaning that they do not participate in the profit and loss of the fund, but they are voting.

MLRO (Money-Laundering Reporting Officer)

An individual who assumes responsibility for all AML and KYC issues. Many regulated entities within Cayman are required to appoint an MLRO, including Excluded managers under SIBL (see Chapter Two).

NAV (Net Asset Value)

The most important number in a fund's books, this is the issue price for new shares, the value of the underlying investments and, therefore, the fund as a whole. NAV's are determined by the administrator and published as frequently, or infrequently, as specified in the PPM.

NFFE (Non-Financial Foreign Institution)

A term defined under FATCA for certain entities that are not required to file information with the IRS because they are not FFI's.

OM (Offering Memorandum)

see PPM.

PEP (Politically Exposed Person)

This is a statutorily defined term that is important for AML purposes. PEP's require greater levels of due diligence in order for a service provider to comply with its AML obligations.

Performance Fee

A fee levied by the investment manager and based on the fund's increase in NAV over a given period. Performance fees generally range between 10 percent and 20 percent per year and are occasionally subject to a hurdle rate (meaning that no performance fee is due unless the fund achieves a return greater than a specific benchmark rate, such as LIBOR, S&P 500, etc.)

PPM (Private Placement Memorandum)

The key document that governs the terms of an investor's investment into an offshore Fund. The PPM is also known as the Offering Document, Off Doc, Offering Memorandum and OM.

Redemption

Shares in a fund are generally not transferable to third parties, but instead the fund allows shareholders to sell their shares back to the fund at the applicable NAV on the date that this takes place. This process is called a redemption.

RO/RA (Registered Office and Registered Agent)

This is the local representative appointed for communication within the Cayman Islands, generally a requirement for all funds that operate there, whether or not incorporated or established in the Cayman Islands.

SEC (Securities and Exchange Commission)

The predominant federal regulator of the funds industry in the United States. (There are others though, such as the CFTC, for example.)

SIBL (Securities Investment Business Law)

Cayman legislation that governs various aspects of the industry, including the licensing of fund managers (see Chapter Two).

SPC (Segregated Portfolio Company)

Also known as segregated cell companies. These are companies capable of creating separate classes (cells, or portfolios) within the company that each enjoys limited liability independent of the rest of the company. See the box on page 86 in Chapter Ten – Fund Structures.

Subscription

When investors subscribe to the fund, they are buying shares.

CPSIA information can be obtained
at www.ICGtesting.com
Printed in the USA
LVXC02n1924291014
411143LV00001B/1

* 9 7 8 0 9 9 0 4 3 6 4 0 9 *